Management
Skills for
New Managers

Management Skills for New Managers

Carol W. Ellis

AMACOM

American Management Association

New York • Atlanta • Brussels • Chicago • Mexico City • San Francisco
Shanghai • Tokyo • Toronto • Washington, D.C.

This publication is designed to provide accurate and authoritative information in regard to the subject matter covered. It is sold with the understanding that the publisher is not engaged in rendering legal, accounting, or other professional service. If legal advice or other expert assistance is required, the services of a competent professional person should be sought.

Various names used by companies to distinguish their software and other products can be claimed as trademarks. AMACOM uses such names throughout this book for editorial purposes only, with no intention of trademark violation. All such software or product names are in initial capital letters or ALL CAPITAL letters. Individual companies should be contacted for complete information regarding trademarks and registration.

Library of Congress Cataloging-in-Publication Data

Ellis, Carol W., 1946 July 13–
    Management skills for new managers / Carol W. Ellis.
        p.   cm.
    Includes bibliographical references and index.
    ISBN 0-8144-0830-3 (pbk.)
    1. Management.   2. Communication in management.   I. Title.

HD31.E552   2004
658—dc22   2004001810

Printing number

10   9   8   7   6   5   4   3

Contents

CHAPTER 5: MOTIVATION 81

CHAPTER 6: DELEGATION FOR GROWTH AND DEVELOPMENT 95

CHAPTER 7: COACHING FOR PERFORMANCE   115

CHAPTER 8: MOVING FORWARD WITH YOUR OWN SITUATIONS   135

Preface

Being a new manager—what a responsibility you have taken on! You may be thinking that the position sounded wonderful when it was offered, and now the reality has set in. You not only have a huge amount of work to accomplish, much more than you did as an individual contributor, but you have all these people who work in your new organization for whom you now have responsibility as well. Where do you start?

The best place to start is to learn how to utilize your direct reports so that you can achieve your necessary results through them. For without them, you will never be successful.

This book, based on the American Management Association's top-selling course, Management Skills for New Managers, is a must read for all new managers. *Management Skills for New Managers* will walk you through the seven required interactive skills for managers so that you can develop knowledge and comfort in working with your direct reports. This book is designed to be used as a workbook to enable you to learn and apply skills such as communicating your new role, coaching a direct report for improved performance, delegating work so that you have time to do those tasks no one else can do, and managing the performance of each one of your direct reports.

Whether you work for a nonprofit, for-profit, educational institute, or the government or own your own business and have employees in that business, the skills introduced in this book will help you to become a more effective manager. As an effective manager using these skills, your direct reports will become more motivated and capable and will help you to achieve your desired results.

Acknowledgments

I would like to express my greatest appreciation to all of the American Management Association faculty members who have taught the seminar, Management Skills for New Managers, upon which this book is based. Over the last few years, they, along with select AMA staff members, have provided new ideas, valuable comments, and useful feedback to make this material most effective.

Also, thanks to my husband, John, and our daughter, Jennifer, who encouraged me to take the challenge of putting my experience in corporate life and my knowledge in developing and delivering management seminars into a book. Without the support of all of these people, I could not have written this book.

Management
Skills for
New Managers

Introduction

As you read this book, you will be introduced to new skills that will—when incorporated into your day-to-day activities—allow you to improve your ability to manage your direct reports. To gain the greatest learning from this process, it is helpful to consider your current work situation, or the new position of manager to which you may aspire, and identify situations that you believe are or will be the most difficult for you to address. These situations might be specific interactions that have generated difficulty for you to achieve success such as letting a direct report know that he needs improvement in his communication with customers or knowing what, when, and to whom to delegate a project. It could even be an event that hasn't yet occurred, but one in which you may anticipate some discomfort, such as delivering a final appraisal.

As you think of your own challenges, write them down on the chart on the following page and then prioritize them in order of importance to your success. In other words, list the most urgent, important, and difficult situations that you want to overcome.

Now that you have identified and prioritized what you want to learn, focus on the top three or four priorities as a foundation for your learning as you read this book. You will be using these challenging situations in your action planning in Chapter 8.

Challenging Situation	Priority
1.	
2.	
3.	
4.	
5.	
6.	
7.	
8.	
9.	
10.	

CHAPTER 1

Defining
Your Role

As we consider the manager's role in today's business environment, it is important to put the subject into the context of what has happened—and is happening—in our world of work, because managers in today's business world can't simply emulate managers of the past and expect the same level of success. The manager's role is more challenging today than in the past because of the numerous changes that are occurring in today's world. These changes are more complex, more frequent, and more rapid than ever before. In this chapter, we will:

❑ Review the business trends that have an impact on management efforts
❑ Clarify the roles and responsibilities of manager
❑ Identify what is needed to create the "right" environment for success

What Is Happening to Our World of Work?

For many managers who entered the workplace in the past ten years, change has been a constant. Those who have been

3

in their world of work for longer than that may remember years of stability, where business processes were constant and change was accomplished over time, not instantaneously. Recognizing that those days are gone in essentially all industries, what do you expect to see in the present and in the future?

Changes will continue to occur at a rapid pace in today's business world. In fact, although many changes have occurred during the past twenty years, we are not stabilized in our workplaces yet. In fact, it is likely that the workplace will never again be *stable* in the traditional definition of the word.

As Joseph H. Boyett and Henry P. Conn describe in their book *Workplace 2000*, "the company that employs the average American in the future will be flatter, leaner, and more aggressive"[1] than it was in the past. The layers of management, supervision, and support that were eliminated in the 1980s and 1990s will not return. Most people have seen that trend in their own companies and in the employers of their friends and families.

Why are companies changing their organizational structures? What is happening in the business world to require the changes we are seeing? What trends affect the roles and responsibilities of managers today?

There are clear and identifiable trends that, once you understand them, will help in defining your workplace environment and the role you have as manager.

Trends in the Business Environment

Following are trends that have affected the businesses of today.

Global Marketplace

The world is a global marketplace with four hubs: North America, Europe, Latin America, and Japan/Asia. Trade agreements such as the North American Free Trade Agreement (NAFTA) are stimulating global trade. Trade opportunities are opening in formerly closed markets such as China, Vietnam, Eastern Europe, and Russia and its Commonwealth states. As more goods and services become available worldwide, developing nations will enter both the industrial and information ages simultaneously, becoming formidable competitors with initially cheap labor pools. They will compete with one another and with the developed economies. The pace of change will also accelerate as the number of producers and buyers in the global economy increases. Businesses today must be organized in a way that will allow them to respond to the implications of this market, typically by becoming flatter with decision making being driven to lower levels than in the past.

U.S. Market

The United States is the single largest market in the world. As such, it is home to domestic- and foreign-based companies. Competition among world-class corporations in the United States continues to spawn layoffs, downsizings, and restructurings that impact America's standard of living and spending power, all which contribute to the leaner organization described previously.

Impact of Information Technology

The transformation of the U.S. economy during the shift from an industrial to an information-based society is as profound as the previous shift from agriculture to industry. Innovations in communications and computer technologies will accelerate the pace of change in the information society. Computers, networks, and massive databases connected worldwide through the Internet will give every individual in the workforce the potential of working wherever they might be—whether at the office, on the road, or at home. Information democratizes management; employees will have access to increasing amounts of information and thus will have the potential of being the managers of their own autonomous businesses—either as part of a larger entity or as independent enterprises. Because of this vast availability of information and the ability to work remotely, managers need to share more information about the work and to trust their employees more than in the past.

Joint Ventures and Strategic Alliances

To cope with the escalating expenses of high-tech research and development, many corporations are forming alliances with related businesses, suppliers, customers, and even competitors (called *coopetition*). These alliances help to bring about new products that might otherwise be impossible to finance; however, these ventures also blur the boundaries between corporate interests and even those of nations. These alliances also challenge the managers involved as different corporate cultures try to work together toward a common goal. Organizations must be open to new ways of doing business and be ready to adopt new processes caused by these changes. Their structures must allow for changes to be made quickly.

Demands for Higher Quality and Faster Service

In the United States, consumer expectations about quality products have been rising at an increasing rate during the past few years. As competition on a global basis intensifies, rival companies will attempt to differentiate themselves and strive for competitive advantages by offering higher quality and faster delivery times. Customers will come to expect both as normal business practices, and then make even more demands. With the rapid dissemination of information, quality standards in one industry quickly become the expectations in others. For example, Nordstrom's legendary customer service is now the benchmark for industries other than retail. Managers must listen to their employees more than ever to determine what customers are experiencing and what changes must be made.

Shorter Product Development Times (Speed to Market)

Companies will need to shorten their turnaround times to meet customer expectations. Manufacturers are beginning to make obsolete their own leading-edge products. For example, Intel constantly innovates to stay ahead of the competition. Massive effort goes into reengineering processes in both the private and public sector to provide faster turnaround on new products and services. This contributes to the aggressiveness of companies today.

Increasing Product Differentiation and Customization

Because of intensifying competition, there will be an increasing demand to individually tailor products and services to the needs of specific customers. That can only be achieved when managers stay close to their customers and learn to anticipate their future needs. Not only managers but also organizations will need to be adaptive and flexible.

External Relations: Customers and Vendors

Because of the reorganizations that are required for companies to be more competitive, nearly everyone will be dealing directly with customers or directly with those who do. Everyone in the organization will be forced to meet customers' needs. Suppliers will be viewed as business partners, rather than as adversaries. Suppliers are already being included in Total Quality Management (TQM) processes to improve quality and reengineer processes to achieve higher productivity. Managers will need to be able to work more effectively and efficiently with people both inside and outside their organizations.

Downsizing and Flatter Hierarchies

Whole layers of management have already been eliminated in many U.S. organizations. With computers providing information to all levels in the organization, the need for layers of managers to process information up and down the hierarchy will diminish. Organizations will continue to flatten the pyramid and experiment with new structures. The only managers who will be needed are those who can:

❑ Add value with their own technical expertise
❑ Serve as coaches to others working with them

Smaller Organizations

In the past, large industrial organizations were seen as the employer of choice and manufacturing drove the U.S. economy. Now, with manufacturing less than 20 percent of the economy, opportunities are emerging for medium- and small-size businesses in the service and information sectors. There are already more people employed in the United States by small female-owned businesses than by all the Fortune 500 Companies combined.

In order to remain lean and flexible to the demands of the marketplace, organizations must continue to outsource as many functions as possible. This will further fuel the growth of small businesses.

Cross-Functional and Self-Managing Teams

As technology on the production line or service site becomes more sophisticated, the need to coordinate decision making and problem solving will become more critical. Most processes are cross-functional in nature, so teams of workers from all functions affected by a process will become more prevalent.

Self-managing teams will share leadership responsibilities so that multiple team members have an opportunity to develop their leadership skills. Managers will be resources for these teams, and they will also serve on teams addressing larger global issues for the organization.

Diversity in the Workforce

The U.S. labor pool is already diverse. By the year 2005, the U.S. Labor Department estimates that 48 percent of the workforce will be female, up from 42 percent in 1980, and 28 percent will be people of color. When the baby boomers begin retiring, the Labor Department predicts that the United States will not have enough trained workers with the skills necessary to fill technical jobs. For the first time since the 1960s, the supply of highly skilled workers will not meet the demand for their services.

Since talent is color and gender blind, organizations that have an established record of offering equal opportunity to all applicants will be in the best position to recruit the best people. That will give them a competitive edge. Managers will need to be able to lead a variety of people. They will need interpersonal skills to bridge gender and cultural differences.

Aging of the Labor Pool

Older workers who have kept their skills current will be encouraged to work part-time rather than retire. Instead of the early retirement programs brought on by the downsizings of the past decade, organizations will be extending the age for full retirement benefits.

Retirement programs will be designed so that employees can take some credit with them if they change jobs because few people will work for the same organization for their entire careers. Organizations and managers will need to be flexible to accommodate this group so that companies can take advantage of the vast amounts of knowledge available through these older workers.

Empowerment of Employees

Because of the growing external demand for higher quality and faster service plus the internal dissemination of information, organizations will need to empower their employees. Managers will delegate responsibility and authority to make their employees more effective. With organizations leaner after downsizing, employees will need to be proficient in their own jobs, understand the jobs of others, and link the two. Organizations will not be able to afford the it's-not-my-job attitudes that prevailed in the past.

Manager as Motivator and Coach

As organizations become leaner and information becomes available to all, a major part of the old-style manager's role will be eliminated. Managers will need to add value to their organizations or their positions will be in jeopardy. Managers will have two roles:

1. Becoming motivators, coaches, and mentors
2. Being responsible for individual projects and serving on teams

For managers to succeed in these roles, they will need strong interpersonal skills and be willing to achieve their own job satisfaction from helping their people develop the skills the organization requires for success.

Lifelong Education and Retraining

The nation's school system is not adequately preparing workers for jobs in the twenty-first century. Major companies such as IBM, Eastman Kodak, Xerox, and Intel, among others, are already working to improve their community school systems. Many companies are finding that they must offer remedial classes in basic skills such as math and reading to bring new employees up to basic standards.

Because of the increasing pace of change in technology, managers will have to commit themselves and their workers to regular ongoing education and training—providing that training will become less expensive because of distance learning capabilities on a variety of media that will allow employees to train at work or at home. Organizations, such as the National Technical University, will be able to provide training by experts in highly specialized fields at reduced costs through technology.

Flexible Hours and Working Conditions

Because of the diversity and aging of the workforce, plus a wide variety of family units with varying needs, organizations in the future will need to be flexible about when workers are physically at work. Technology will support many workers' ability to work almost anywhere. Managers will need to manage a variety of work arrangements in order to keep the talent they need on their teams.

More organizations will offer day care and on-site schools for employee's children. Hewlett Packard, Honeywell, Martin Marietta, and American Bankers Insurance Group already have on-site schools for their employees' children. In order to be competitive, other companies will need to start offering similar benefits.

As people begin to live longer, more employees will have the responsibility for elder care; companies will respond by offering elder care support programs. Workers will choose from cafeteria-style benefit plans and have the ability to change their benefits as their needs change. Companies must respond to the expectations of their employee base for health care packages, flexible working hours, or any of the other benefits, or the workers will move to companies that provide the preferred benefits.

Healthy Orientation

Organizations will become more involved with the health of their employees in an effort to keep health care costs down. Employees will be asked to share an increasing amount of health care costs. Incentives will be offered for quitting smoking, maintaining a healthy diet, and exercising. Managers will need to take the time to be knowledgeable about and sensitive to the health needs of their employees.

The Environment

Recycling will become profitable and organizations will be eager to show the public their concern for the environment by using and advertising their use of recycled materials. Manufacturers will perform environmental background checks to ensure that the components of their products have not been manufactured with processes harmful to the environment. Intel and Hewlett Packard are already doing this as a part of their supplier selection process.

Packaging will be streamlined to reduce waste because the consumer will demand it. To respond to these demands, companies will need to be organized in a way that promotes innovation and responds to customer expectations.

The Impact of These Changes

As these trends indicate, customers now expect and demand quick turnaround on services and products. In fact, the current expectation of most workers is also to be able to have what they need when they need it.

Companies that have become smaller and flatter are often better able to respond to these immediate needs by having a quicker decision-making process than they had in the past. Their reduction in size has allowed them to speed their processes so that they are better able to meet these market demands. Many companies attribute the ability to accomplish and maintain this flattening, in part, to the introduction of improved technology. Technology is also a driver in the need for workers to stay up-to-date with their skills and to improve their decision-making abilities.

This trend of speeding up requires all employees to perform at high levels in the following areas: problem solving, developing improved ways to work, thinking creatively, and working effectively in a group. No longer can workers be complacent about their skills and no longer can managers assume that their direct reports have the skills to do their work without support.

What Changes Have You Seen in Your Company That Affect You in Your Role as a Manager?

_____

_____

_____

_____

_____

_____

The Role of Today's Manager in an Ever-Changing Environment

The role of today's manager is even more complicated because of today's ever-changing environment. Today's manager must be able to deal with the complexity and speed of change that is occurring in the organization. Managers of previous generations did not have to deal with the rapidity, complexity, and frequency of changes that today's manager must handle.

In addition to these changes, a transition to management means that you give up your role as an individual contributor. When you were an individual contributor in the organization, your success was measured by the accomplishment of your own work. If you did your tasks, you were successful and were rewarded in many ways.

As a manager, you are no longer responsible for what you alone accomplish. You now must work with your direct reports to achieve the goals of your department and your organization.

In order to fully understand the difference between the roles and responsibilities of individual contributors and managers, make a list of the responsibilities you had as an individual contributor.

Now, list your managerial responsibilities:

_____

_____

_____

_____

_____

In comparing the two lists, it should become apparent that:

The Manager's Role Is to Achieve Results Through and With Others

Your role is to work with other people, to help them be productive and effective. Your ability to work with your people and to understand their needs and abilities will directly impact your ability to achieve results through them. As a manager, you will need to play many roles—and your ability to play these roles will directly determine your effectiveness as a manager. Let's look at the typical roles you will have to be able to play in order to *achieve results with and through other people.*

Eight Typical Roles of Effective Managers

1. **Leader.** The leader looks beyond the current day-to-day work requirements and determines where her organization needs to go. Leaders move their organizations forward by thinking strategically about the directions they need to take. They form relationships beyond the organization to build and maintain the reputation of the organization.

Give an example of someone using the **leader** role:

_____

_____

_____

2. **Director.** The director is able to define a problem and take the initiative to determine a solution. Using planning and goal-setting skills, the director determines what to delegate and ensures that individuals understand what they are being asked to do.

Give an example of someone using the **director** role:

_____

_____

_____

3. **Contributor.** The contributor is expected to be task oriented and work focused, ensuring that his own personal productivity is attended to along with motivating others to be sure that their organization's productivity is at its highest potential.

Give an example of someone using the **contributor** role:

_____

_____

_____

4. **Coach.** The coach is engaged in the development of people by creating a caring, empathetic orientation: being helpful, considerate, sensitive, approachable, open, and fair.

Give an example of someone using the **coach** role:

_____

_____

_____

5. **Facilitator.** The facilitator fosters a collective effort for the organization, building cohesion and teamwork, and managing interpersonal conflict.

Give an example of someone using the **facilitator** role:

_____

_____

_____

6. **Observer.** The observer pays attention to what is going on in the unit, determining if people are meeting their objectives, and watching to see that the unit is meeting its goals. The observer is also responsible for understanding what is important for the team to know and ensuring that information overload does not occur.

Give an example of someone using the **observer** role:

_____

_____

_____

7. **Innovator.** The innovator facilitates adaptation and change, paying attention to the changing environment, identifying trends impacting the organization, and, then, determining needed changes for the success of the organization.

Give an example of someone using the **innovator** role:

_____

_____

_____

8. **Organizer.** The organizer takes responsibility for planning work, organizing tasks and structures, and then following up to ensure that what is committed to is completed by attending to technological needs, staff coordination, crisis handling, and so forth.

Give an example of someone using the **organizer** role:

_____

_____

_____

Ways to Create the Right Environment

One of the primary responsibilities of your role as manager is to create the right environment—the one that will help you to achieve the results you want through others. For many of you, your managers and their peers operated in a directive style, telling you what to do and then closely supervising you as you carried out the directive. We know that some direction is necessary, but the "just telling" model no longer works in our current environment of global competition, growing technology, and demanding consumers. The competencies needed now for successful management include guiding, supporting, and developing others to higher levels of performance.

Effective managers now respond to these challenges by creating an environment in which individuals are motivated to perform. This ideal environment includes:

❑ Setting clear expectations (understood by both the direct report and the manager) for the work to be completed

❑ Observing the direct report's behavior to determine if there is sufficient knowledge, skill, and motivation for the individual to complete the task

❑ Knowing each individual's needs and drivers

❑ Delegating effectively to all of your direct reports

❑ Coaching each individual for improved performance

❑ Working effectively with your peers or team

When you create the right environment, achieving results through others becomes much easier. Your role as a manager is to help create the right motivational environment to ensure your department's success.

Obstacles to Creating the Right Environment

Creating the right environment is critical to your management success; however, there are two potential barriers the new manager must effectively deal with in order to ensure success:

Managing Former Peers

One of the most difficult aspects of being a new manager is having to manage those people who were formerly your peers. Don't be surprised if your peers express jealousy or resentment—they may have applied for the very job that you got! Be objective, be fair, and be focused on making the most of your new career opportunity and confirming higher management's opinion that you were indeed the best candidate for the job.

The following ideas will help you during this transition:

❑ Clearly explain your new role and how you will be working with them in this role.
❑ Don't show favoritism.
❑ Encourage them to provide ideas on how the team can work together and use their ideas whenever possible.
❑ Validate their feelings—for example, by saying, "I know it may be difficult for you to work for me."
❑ Ask how they would like to work with you.
❑ Don't fall into the "but you used to be one of the guys" trap.
❑ Keep working hard to show why you got the job.

After considering these suggestions, write those actions you can take to ease your situation:

_____

_____

_____

_____

_____

Establishing Expectations with Your Manager

Disagreements or misunderstandings between your manager and you about your role and responsibilities can undermine your effectiveness as a new manager. You need to know what your manager expects from you and from your direct reports in order to deliver successful results. We will be looking at some specifics regarding expectations later in this book. And we'll explore some ideas on effectively communicating with your manager.

Knowing and developing your own skills is one part of

being a manager. Another part is, as we have discussed, knowing your role and being flexible when interacting with your direct reports. Next, we will explore the importance of communicating effectively, so that you are able to deliver your messages in a way that the recipient can take positive action to meet your needs.

With all the changes that are occurring in the workplace, and the demands these changes and the change in your role from individual contributor to manager make on you, your success will depend on understanding what the company, your customers (internal or external), and your direct reports need from you. Once you understand what they need, you can adapt your thoughts and chosen interactions to create the greatest opportunity for everyone to be successful. The remaining chapters in this book will give you that knowledge and introduce you to the skills that will help you to achieve success.

Note

1. Boyette, Joseph H., and Henry P. Conn, *Workplace 2000* (New York: Plume, 1992).

Action Planning Notes

In order to achieve success with your performance as a manager and to have a successful team, it is important to consider what actions you will take at work. This will become the foundation for the final activity in this book.

You will be encouraged to take a few minutes after reading and working on the material in each chapter to write down thoughts and actions that you will take with your direct reports for mutual success (see the worksheet on the following page).

Some examples are:

❑ Identify learning phases for each task for each direct report.

❑ Provide support and direction based on the learning phases.

❑ Delegate the agenda for staff meetings.

❑ Provide useful feedback on work through effective coaching.

❑ Clarify expectations.

❑ Break down production of the annual data report into smaller components (for those who are motivated by achievement).

Take a few minutes to identify where there have been misunderstandings or difficulties with any of your direct reports or your manager. What action will you take to address these situations?

Individual	Action

CHAPTER 2

Effective Communication

The foundation of all relationships is communication. Without communicating effectively, we are not able to achieve our goals and objectives. With that in mind, this chapter will look at:

❑ The best application of the different modes of communication
❑ The tools and skills necessary for effective communication
❑ The best ways to communicate your organizational goals
❑ The most effective use of e-mail
❑ Managing the relationship with your manager through improved communication
❑ Running effective meetings

Communicating with Your Staff

Most new managers are accustomed to communicating laterally and upward. And you probably do quite well in that area.

After all, you have been using this skill as a component of your daily work life as an individual contributor. You certainly have talked successfully with your manager or you wouldn't have been promoted. And, no doubt, you've had many opportunities to interact and communicate with your peers. However, your skill at communicating downward to your direct reports may not yet be fully developed, because you haven't had direct reports before.

Why is it so important that you develop a high degree of competence in downward communication? The answer is to help your direct reports become successful.

Your Direct Reports Will Have More Influence on Your Success Than Any Other Group or Individual

Their ability to function and be successful at their work speaks to how well you are able to communicate, interact, and guide them.

Too many new managers spend most of their time planning upward communication. They worry about what the boss thinks of them, believing that he is the most important person to please. They give little thought to the people who really control their future. Communicating to your direct reports is probably new for you, and it might be uncomfortable for you. But as a new manager, one of the keys to your success lies in your ability to effectively communicate with your employees.

One of the most common complaints of direct reports is that their new manager doesn't keep them informed. They feel ignored and undervalued. Too often, neglected communication is not done on purpose, but is created, rather, by omission. Communication, if not planned, becomes just a victim of circumstances.

The first step in planning to improve communication is to recognize what is important for you to communicate. Let's look at what kinds of information you may need to communicate to your staff and then we'll examine how this is best accomplished.

What You Need to Communicate

In your role as manager, you need to communicate many different types of information to many different people inside and outside of the organization.

You are expected to keep your staff informed about many different areas of the business in which you had had little involvement before. For instance, if there is a change in personnel policy, you may need to be the bearer of the news. Or, if there is a change in your reporting structure, you will be the one who has the responsibility to advise your staff. Certainly, you need to let your staff know your goals and objectives. And you have the responsibility to coach your direct reports for improved or expanded performance.

Let's look at some of the information you will be communicating:

❑ Procedures
❑ Project information
❑ Scheduled meetings
❑ Conference calls
❑ Team objectives and goals
❑ Employee performance

What Other Information Do You Need to Communicate?

_____

_____

_____

_____

_____

The Communication Process

Communication occurs regularly in an organization. To understand why some verbal communications are more successful than others, it is important to recognize the components of this skill.

In the model in Figure 2-1, the sender develops a message. This message is developed or encoded using the experience, value, attitudes, language, knowledge, gender, age, and so forth of the sender. The filters that are used in encoding the sender's message are often unconscious influences in the way we say or write things.

The receiver hears and sees (through the body language) the message, and using the same elements from her own perspective, interprets or decodes the message. The interpretation is based on similar but unique filters.

In successful communication, the receiver provides feedback based on what he believes the message to be. This feedback can be in the form of verbal information or body language.

Some common filters are:

❑ Believing that younger workers don't know what they are doing (age)

❑ Believing that older workers can't learn new ways of doing things (age)

❑ Interpreting the actual words said differently than was intended (not speaking the same "language")

Figure 2-1. The communication process.

What Filters Are Present with You and Your Coworkers?

_____

_____

_____

_____

_____

What and How to Communicate

As a manager, it is important when thinking about what you have to communicate that you consider not only what filters may be in place but also how much information you need to share. Because you are often very busy and are trying to get many things done at once, you may think that people only need to know what is happening or will be happening without giving any explanation for the situation. You may think: Why should I have to give them more information than they need? However, depending on the receiver's filters and perspective, too little information may cause a negative reaction.

Information is a valuable component of communication. Through providing sufficient information regarding an action requested, everyone is able to make more accurate interpretations of the message.

Note the difference between the following two statements:

1. "All team members will work overtime until further notice."
2. "Due to the latest information on the market opportunities for this latest toy, it will be necessary for all team members to work overtime for the next ten days to get the design completed. Thanks for your cooperation."

The first statement is likely to create resistance. The receivers of this message have no idea why you are telling them to work overtime or how long they are expected to work these extra hours. Many questions, at least in their minds, will be asked. Team members will spend time discussing the message and speculating on the answers to their questions.

While the second statement takes about seven seconds longer to deliver, the clarity of it allows receivers to hear it and have at least some of their questions answered. They will hear and accept it with less resistance.

Paying attention to the words selected and the way in which they will be received is critical for effective communication.

Once the message has been delivered, look and ask for feedback. Feedback can be verbal or visual, and it is necessary. It is the only way that you can be certain that the message you have developed is the one that is received.

Communication Components

Everyone communicates all the time. We can't help it. Even when we say nothing, we are communicating. When working toward effective communication, it is important to understand what effect the various components of communication have on our success.

What is it that makes one way to communicate better than another? There are times when we get a reaction that we don't expect. What causes that?

When we break down the components, we can see that there are three major elements involved:

1. *Verbal.* The words we choose.
2. *Vocal.* The way we say them, such as tone, pitch, or volume of voice.
3. *Visual.* Body language, facial expressions, eye movement, gesturing.

Each of these components provides a part of the overall effectiveness of communication. If you are able to use all three parts, you will have the greatest chance to be understood. When you are able to use only one or two, you will have the greatest chance to be misunderstood.

Let's look at the options we have in our methods of communicating.

Communication Methods

There are several accepted methods of communicating information to those around you. Depending on the topic, one way may be more preferable and effective to use. When you use appropriate methods, your chances for successful communication are significantly improved. There are basically three ways of communicating:

1. *In Person.*

   ❑ To another person
   ❑ To several people in a group (team)
   ❑ To many people in a large group (public speaking)

   This method allows all three of the components (verbal, vocal, visual) of communication to be used. When there is sensitive information, or information that affects an individual's personal or career life, it should be done in person. If questions arise in the interpretation of the message, you will be able to see those questions through body language, and the receiver of the message will be able to see your body language and better understand your message. Communicating in person can be to one or more people, but always includes the visual element.

   In What Situations Would You Use This Method?

   _____

   _____

_____

_____

_____

2. *Voice Only.*

    ❑ Telephone
    ❑ Voice mail
    ❑ Recorded messages

    Voice-only communication is very effective when you have information that you need to receive or deliver and it is not of a sensitive nature, for instance, information on a project or schedule changes. In this method of communicating, you are able to tell from the tone of voice if there is doubt or questions regarding your message. Similarly, the receiver can determine part of your message, such as happiness or frustration, through your tone of voice. While the visual element isn't available for interpretation, voice-only communication is still quite effective for some messages.

    In What Situations Would You Use This Method?

    _____

    _____

    _____

    _____

    _____

3. *Written.*

   ❑ Memos
   ❑ Formal letters
   ❑ Instruction manuals
   ❑ E-mail

The last method, and the communication most likely to be misinterpreted, is written. Without the tone of voice (vocal) and body language (visual) elements, the receiver has only his own filters to use in interpretation. This method is most effectively used when detail is required and procedures are to be followed. Additionally, many of our business efforts need to be captured in writing, often as a follow-up to a conversation or documentation of agreements.

In What Situations Would You Use This Method?

_____

_____

_____

_____

Among the most common forms of written communication is e-mail. Because we often use e-mail in lieu of talking with someone, we treat it as a casual communication channel. What we might say in person to someone is now said in writing, without the benefit of the vocal and visual clues that are so important to correct interpretation. Let's take a look at some guidelines for the effective use of e-mail.

How to Use E-Mail Effectively

The use of e-mail as a form of business communication is on the rise. As more people begin using this medium, it becomes increasingly important to consider:

❑ What to send
❑ How to word the message
❑ To whom to send it

What to Send

We have identified the information that can best be delivered in writing. Consider now which of those pieces of information is best delivered via e-mail. In addition to the formal information that is sent using this technology, e-mail is also used to communicate in a more informal manner. This is where misunderstandings can occur. Be sure that the message you are sending is appropriate to send in writing.

What Messages Can Be Sent via E-Mail?

_____

_____

_____

_____

_____

What Messages Cannot Be Sent via E-Mail?

_____

_____

_____

_____

Remember, e–mail is a permanent record and can be forwarded to others and can be used as evidence in a court of law.

How to Word the Message

When we consider the impact of the various components of communication—verbal, vocal, and visual—it is easy to realize how, even with the best of intentions, misunderstandings can occur. Certainly, these misunderstandings occur in all forms of communication, but e-mail exacerbates these situations because we use e-mail as a form of informal communication (as when we speak to one another), but it is one way, not interactive in real time. Because we are not able to read the visual clues that occur when we are speaking with another person, e-mail lends itself to misinterpretation.

Being a one-way communication channel eliminates the opportunity for speaker and listener to identify confusion during the communication process. Typically in other forms of discussion, we are able to see or hear this confusion and can alleviate it with additional information or different body language or tone of voice.

It is imperative, therefore, that consideration be taken to ensure that we send the message from the perspective of the receiver. That is to say, that we word e-mails so that regardless of the mood or situation of the receiver, the message is delivered as we intend.

To Whom to Send the Message

E-mail messages often are sent as broadcast messages to many people. The reason for this is typically that these people might be interested. Unless this person who might be interested is your manager, consider whether the people really need to see the message. Even when it does include your manager, consider her need to know.

Hours of time are spent in businesses throughout the world opening, reading, and acting on e-mails. Many of these hours are unnecessarily spent as the messages are not relevant to the recipient. You can influence this by taking special consideration in addressing your e-mail messages to include only those who have a need to know.

As you become discriminating in your addressees, you can also become influential in minimizing unwanted e-mail directed to you by responding to the sender and asking him to eliminate you from his list for that topic.

Netiquette (Network Etiquette)

Because e-mail is permanent and can easily be forwarded, it is important to take care in composing the message. This message becomes an image of you, and in a work situation, you want that image to be positive. Take the time to pay attention to the details of punctuation, spelling, and grammar.

In addition to the basics of English grammar, there are certain *netiquette* guidelines for the best use of the Internet and intranets. Included in these guidelines are admonitions to:

❑ Think before you write.
❑ Avoid "flaming" or expressing extreme emotion.
❑ Avoid using all caps (this is the equivalent of screaming).
❑ Read your messages carefully before sending them.
❑ Stick to your subject.

How to Communicate the Change in Your Role

Another communication challenge many new managers have is related to the change in your status. For instance, your promotion has been a change for you, your direct reports, and your manager—actually, for everyone who interacts with you at work. You have a changed role and different responsibilities. Letting people know what will be different with your new role is critical to achieving a common understanding of the new relationships created by your promotion.

In order to understand how this might be affecting you, take a few minutes to think of those people with whom you now have a changed relationship (your former peers, your old manager, your customers, and so forth). Answer the following questions for each of these people:

Person 1
❑ Who is the individual?

❑ What is the nature of the change in your relationship?

❑ How has the new relationship been addressed?

❑ What impact has there been on you and the others?

Person 2
❑ Who is the individual?

❑ What is the nature of the change in your relationship?

❑ How has the new relationship been addressed?

❑ What impact has there been on you and the others?

Person 3
❑ Who is the individual?

❑ What is the nature of the change in your relationship?

❑ How has the new relationship been addressed?

❑ What impact has there been on you and the others?

Person 4
❑ Who is the individual?

❑ What is the nature of the change in your relationship?

❑ How has the new relationship been addressed?

❑ What impact has there been on you and the others?

Understanding What the Change Means to You and Others

Why is it so difficult for some people to change? The answer lies in understanding what happens during the transition from the old way to the new way. When individuals realize that the change is going to affect them, they often experience fear of the unknown. As a manager, how you help those affected by change will influence their ability to progress to the new way.

What can you do? The most important element for long-term success is to understand that it is difficult for many people. Once you understand that, then how and what you communicate can make the transition easier.

Some communication guidelines include the following tips:

❑ Acknowledge the difficulty they may be experiencing.
❑ Create opportunities for short-term successes.
❑ Praise achievements.
❑ Clearly identify the "new way"—that is, your new relationship to them.
❑ Make yourself available often, perhaps by walking around the workplace.
❑ Talk to your direct reports about upcoming change when possible.
❑ Involve your staff in decisions about changes if appropriate.

It is also best to keep the number of simultaneous changes to a minimum. Too many changes create chaos, which is debilitating. Try to get one change accepted before overlaying another.

By using these guidelines, and taking into consideration the difficulty others may have with change, you can increase your probability of success greatly. Remember, not everyone is excited about the changes that happen at work. Helping them become comfortable with a climate of change is part of your management responsibility.

Return to the individuals you identified who are affected by your new role, and identify what you will now do to improve the understanding of the new relationship.

Person 1:

Person 2:

Person 3:

Person 4:

How Will You Make Changes?

Now consider what changes you may need to make in your organization or on your team. These changes may be procedural, organizational, assignments, or other changes. Select one of these changes that you will be making and identify how specifically you will communicate and implement that change:

The Change I Am Making

_____

_____

_____

How I Will Communicate the Change

_____

_____

_____

_____

How I Will Implement the Change

_____

_____

_____

_____

Managing Your Relationship with Your Manager Through Improved Communication

An important skill for the new manager is the ability to manage up. Often you are caught between your manager and his thinking versus your own thinking and that of your staff. It is easy to assume that the person who promoted you has more knowledge and better ideas than you do; however, he or she may not have knowledge about the people who report to you or the work in which you are currently involved.

Your managers will often ask you to take on a new task or to redirect your efforts toward something that has suddenly become important to them. How can you meet their needs while not sacrificing the goals that you have established with your own team?

When communicating with your manager, you must begin with thinking about "What's in it for her?" or "Why does he care?'' Doing that will help you to focus on the most effective way of putting together information so that your manager will be able to relate to the impact of your information.

EXAMPLE:

For instance, suppose your boss asks you to cut your budget by 10 percent. A typical response would be to say you would comply and then go back to your desk and take a hard look at how to do that. However, if you know that a budget cut will affect your team's ability to meet its objectives for the year, it would be better to go to your boss and ask for more information about the priorities of your objectives and what must be retained and what can be delayed or eliminated. By doing this, you get your boss to buy into the new priorities or possibly reduce the cut that must be made.

Answering the concerns about ''What's in it for her?'' or ''Why does he care?'' reveals the boss needs to reduce his budget. That is clear. However, he must understand what that does to the work of your team, and ultimately to his performance for the year.

How to Use Communication to Manage Your Manager

Think of a situation when your manager has asked you to:

❑ Do something that will interfere with the plans you have already established with your team
❑ Do something that you disagree with

Develop a communication plan to work on with this manager for resolving the differences.

What Is the Request from Your Manager?

_____

_____

_____

_____

_____

What Impact Will It Have on You and Your Organization?

_____

_____

_____

_____

_____

What Will You Communicate? (List the key points—remember to think from your manager's perspective.)

_____

_____

_____

_____

_____

_____

How Will You Communicate It? (In person, on the telephone, in writing, or a combination of these)

_____

_____

_____

_____

_____

When Will the Communication Occur?

_____

_____

_____

_____

_____

How to Run Effective Meetings

Another major component to include in effective communications is that of communicating in meetings. Undoubtedly one of your responsibilities as a manager is to run meetings. Most of us have had a great deal of experience attending meetings, and we may have had the opportunity to run some meetings.

Some of the meetings we attended or ran were probably very well run, while others may have been disorganized and inefficient. What was it that made the difference?

Some common complaints about meetings include:

❑ Starting late
❑ Not having a purpose
❑ No clear objective for the meeting
❑ Disorganized
❑ Some attendees don't participate
❑ Some attendees do all the talking
❑ Longer than they need to be
❑ No common understanding of the results

Approaching the meeting in a logical, organized manner will help to ensure its success. There are four steps you can take to help ensure that your meeting is effective:

1. Planning the meeting
2. Announcing the meeting
3. Conducting the meeting
4. Evaluating the meeting

Planning the Meeting

The first step in having a successful meeting is to plan for it. With this plan, you organize your thoughts so that you can achieve your meeting goals.

Consider the following items in your planning:

Purpose:	What results do you want from the meeting?
Agenda:	What will be discussed? In what order? In how much depth?
Length:	When should the meeting be held? How long should it last?
Attendees:	Who should attend? Make sure the right individuals are included.
Evaluation:	How will you know the meeting has been successful?

Announcing the Meeting

After the planning has been completed and prior to the meeting day, send a memo to let people know what they should be prepared to discuss in the meeting. Having an agenda helps everyone to plan for the meeting and keeps them focused on the meeting's purpose. Include in your advance agenda additional information that will help to prepare others for their participation in the meeting.

Use the following PAL format to let people know of the meeting.

Please plan to attend a staff meeting in the conference room on:

Tuesday, June 24 at 10:00 AM. Be prepared to discuss the following topic in detail. Please bring all ideas with you.

Purpose: To develop a process to introduce the new software system to the entire organization.

Agenda:
1. Introductions
2. Current status of the software system
3. Discussion of the process required for the introduction
4. Identification of who will be involved
5. Development of target dates
6. Assignment of responsibilities
7. Next steps
8. Meeting evaluation

Length: 4 hours. Lunch will be provided.

Conducting an Effective Meeting

When running a meeting, it is important to remember that this is not an opportunity for you to do an information dump. All participants want and need a chance to talk about their ideas and help develop solutions for the meeting's purpose. We often get so caught up in our own agendas that we forget to take a breath and ask other people for their thoughts.

Here are some tips for effective meetings:

❑ *Start the meeting with some general information about the purpose.* This gives everyone the same foundation from which to begin the communication.

❑ *Establish "meeting-keeping" roles such as timekeeper, agenda cop, scribe, and moderator.* This will help ensure that the meeting runs smoothly and that meeting notes will be available for everyone.

❑ *Introduce the use of a "parking lot."* When a participant introduces a topic that is not on the agenda, have her put the thought on a Post-it Note and place the Post-it on the parking lot (a piece of paper taped on the wall with the words *parking lot* at the top of it). In this way, the thought is acknowledged and not forgotten.

❑ *Follow the agenda.*

❑ *Generate discussion among all attendees.* Ways to do this include:

—Asking for feedback

—Asking another attendee to paraphrase what was just said

—Encouraging participation by asking quiet attendees what they think

—Reflecting on what you think is being said or thought

—Supporting participant ideas

❑ *Recap the outcomes or results of the meetings.* Make sure that each attendee knows the action expected of him/her based on the meeting.

❑ *Meet your time commitments.* If the meeting is running late, ask participants if they are able to extend the time, or reschedule the meeting continuation for another time.

❑ *Review "parking lot" items.* If possible within the originally scheduled time, address these concerns. If time will not permit, ask if another meeting needs to be scheduled with these items on the agenda.

❑ *Set a time for a next meeting.*

❑ *Ask for a meeting evaluation.* This ensures that participants have an opportunity to let you know what worked well in the meeting and what they would like to see done differently.

Evaluating the Meeting

You may elect to request evaluations at the conclusion of the meeting. If time does not permit, you may send out an evaluation form to all attendees. It is critical that you get feedback from all attendees so that you have a clear picture of others' perceptions of the meeting's effectiveness.

Following is a meeting evaluation form that you may use to help you improve your meeting skills. Note that these forms do not have space for a name. In order to get honest feedback from individuals you manage, it is sometimes necessary to have the feedback provided anonymously.

Meeting Evaluation

From your perspective, please respond to the following statements/questions about this meeting. Your answers will provide information for continual improvement of these meetings.

1. The purpose of the meeting was clearly stated at the beginning of the meeting.   Yes   No

2. The meeting's agenda was available to all attendees.   Yes   No

3. The agenda was followed during the meeting.   Yes   No

4. The meeting's objectives were met.   Yes   No

5. Were your personal objectives met?   Yes   No

6. Everyone was encouraged to actively participate in the meeting.   Yes   No

7. What part of the meeting was most valuable to you?

_____

_____

8. Which part of the meeting was the least valuable to you?

_____

_____

9. What recommendations do you have for conducting future meetings?

_____

_____

Those Times of Miscommunication

Even with your best efforts and understanding of effective communication, there may be times when you are misunderstood. When this happens, acknowledge the misunderstanding, ask for clarification of what the individual understands of the message, and attempt to correct the misunderstanding. Because of the varied filters we all have and our preferred method of getting information (verbal, in writing, or by example in person), it is critical to the successful communication process that effective feedback is used by both the sender and receiver.

Action Planning Notes

Remember, in order to achieve success with your performance as a manager and to have a successful team, it is important
to take the time to consider what actions you will take at work.
This will become the foundation for the final activity in this
book.

Some examples are:

❑ Discuss my new role with my customer and how the relationship will work in the future.

❑ Develop and distribute a PAL before my next staff
meeting.

Where has communication broken down within your work
group? Identify what action you will take to mend that. This
could include communicating with particular people, managing
your manager, improving your e-mail effectiveness, or running
meetings.

Individual	Action

CHAPTER 3

Performance Management

We have introduced the concept that a manager's primary responsibility is to achieve results through others. And we have explored the importance of effective communication. Our next step is to investigate the process of managing the performance and development of your direct reports. We will do that by focusing on the following:

❑ Knowing your responsibilities in managing others' performance
❑ Compiling a typical personnel file
❑ Understanding the performance management process
❑ Setting expectations that will achieve results

Performance Management

Most companies have their own system for managing the performance of their employees. The information in this chapter can be used in support of any plan. You are encouraged to overlay what you learn in this book with the system you use at work.

What Is Performance Management?

❑ Ongoing process of working with your direct reports in a partnership for the purpose of helping them (and you) to be successful

❑ Ongoing communication for the benefit of the organization and the individual

❑ Ongoing process punctuated by formal quarterly review sessions

What Isn't It?

❑ A once-a-year appraisal

❑ An opportunity to punish your direct reports

The Goal of Performance Management

Effective performance management is the avenue for achieving organizational goals, which impact the business's bottom line. By mastering this important skill, you will be able to create a greater alignment of the organization's interest and interests of the individual employee, as shown in Figure 3-1.

The Performance Management Plan

As we have noted, different companies have different forms and processes to follow. As a manager, it is imperative that you adhere to the plans of your company.

Most companies set expectations or objectives at the beginning, or near the beginning, of the year. Some of these are set top down, and others are set from the individual contributor level up. However your company sets objectives, it is important that your direct reports agree to those that they will own.

Review periods are also set by policy in most companies.

Figure 3-1. The goal of performance management.

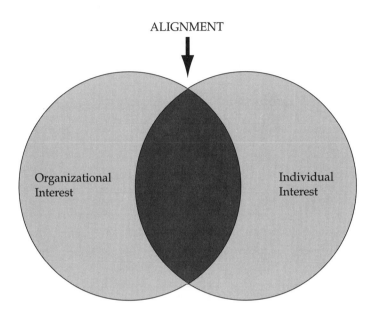

Some will require only an annual review; others will require two, three, or four reviews annually. Regardless of the number of required reviews in your company, you may choose to hold more performance discussions than that number.

Experts in the performance management field recommend that reviews be held at least quarterly so that the individual has the opportunity to get back on track if he or she has strayed off course.

Why Should Managers Hold Quarterly Discussions?

Some of the common reasons for holding quarterly discussions include:

❑ It provides an opportunity to discuss performance in a routine manner.
❑ Direct reports become comfortable participating in these performance discussions since they are routine.

❑ Problems are discovered before it's too late to fix them.

❑ Managers become more comfortable holding these performance discussions.

❑ Direct reports can have their objectives updated.

What Other Reasons Can You Identify?

_____

_____

_____

_____

_____

_____

_____

Have You Identified the Challenges?

Often, the most difficult step to take in putting together performance management plans is the first step. That step is to set objectives or expectations. The next big challenge comes in having review meetings.

Why is there reluctance among so many managers to work on performance management plans? Some of the reasons often stated are:

❑ I don't have time.

❑ I don't know what they do.

❑ It's just an administrative requirement.

❑ It's not an important part of my job.

What Other Reasons Do You Know?

_____

_____

_____

_____

_____

_____

Whose Responsibility Is It?

Clearly, with all the reasons previously stated, the process can often be overwhelming, especially for the new manager. In fact, many managers think that they must do all the work in the development of the performance management plan. But when responsibilities are shared between the manager and the direct report, it becomes much more approachable. No manager should feel that he is operating independently when it comes to an individual's performance. After all, it is the individual's job that is being affected and the individual needs to take ownership for her success in that job.

In companies that have effective performance management plans, the managers are typically responsible for, among other things:

❑ Initiating the conversations about the plan
❑ Identifying the top-down objectives
❑ Ensuring that responsibilities for the group's work are fairly distributed

The employee accepting the performance management plan also has responsibilities. Those include, but are not limited to:

❑ Clearly understanding what is expected
❑ Letting the manager know when objectives are unrealistic
❑ Establishing his own specific objectives within the boundaries set by the manager
❑ Writing her own developmental objectives

Activity: Whose Responsibility Is It?

Thinking about your own company's performance management process, write down all of the responsibilities you have as manager, and then all of the responsibilities of your direct reports.

The Manager's Responsibility

_____

_____

_____

_____

_____

_____

_____

_____

The Direct Report's Responsibility

_____

_____

_____

_____

_____

_____

_____

_____

_____

When responsibilities are shared and expectations are jointly set, your direct reports will be more committed to achieving those expectations. Include them to get their greatest work.

Let's look now at how to set expectations that are written so that they are clearly understood.

Setting Objectives

An important element in a performance management plan, and certainly the one that must be the initial effort, is the set of objectives that becomes the agreement for work between the manager and the direct report. These expectations need to be written clearly so that there is a specific target for the direct report to work toward.

Well-written objectives follow the format of:

S—Specific = Exactly what is expected from the direct report? This must be stated clearly so that both direct report and manager will know what needs to be done.

M—Measurable = How will the individual know that he or she has achieved the desired outcome? Of what is the measurement indicative? How will you gather the results?

A—Attainable = Is the objective realistic, attainable, and appropriate for the individual in that position?

R—Relevant = Are the desired results relevant for the individual, given knowledge, skills, experience, internal and external conditions, and so forth?

T—Trackable = How will progress be tracked? Is there a time frame for achievement? **Timebound** = By when must the objective be completed?

Once the objectives are written and agreed upon, tracking the results of these becomes an ongoing process. Remembering that the purpose of the performance management process is for the direct report and manager to be successful, a review of the progress in meeting the objectives provides the opportunity for the direct report to ask for support and the manager to understand what she can do to help the individual achieve the required results.

Examples of Well-Written Objectives

❑ Increase sales of project management software applications by 10 percent by year's end

❑ Train five departments on the use of the new expense reimbursement process in the third quarter of this year

❑ Reduce data entry errors from previous quarterly results by 3 percent each quarter of this year

❑ Complete six days of training by end of year

Activity: Setting Objectives

In order to completely understand this format:

❑ Think of one of your own or one of your direct reports' objectives and write it here in the SMART format.

S—What is it specifically that you need to have accomplished?

_____

_____

_____

_____

M—How will you measure the objective? How will the individual know that he has achieved what you expect?

_____

_____

_____

_____

A—Is the objective attainable by this person? This information does not have to be included in the objective, but you must answer this question before you hold the individual responsible for accomplishing it.
(yes or no)

_____

R—Is the objective relevant to the work of the individual? Again this information does not have to be included in the objective, but you must answer this before you hold the individual responsible for accomplishing it. Identify in what way it is relevant.
(yes or no)

_____

T—When does the objective have to be completed? And how will you track the results?

_____

_____

_____

_____

❑ Write your objective in one sentence including the S, M, and T elements. Use the previous examples as a guideline.

_____

_____

_____

_____

You may find that you will struggle with the measurement element. Many positions have responsibilities that are difficult to measure. If you want to have the objective met, however, it is imperative that you determine how the person will know what she is expected to do. For instance, if your group is a technical support organization, your direct reports may be responsible for responding to incoming calls. Identifying call volumes, call length, or customer satisfaction may be necessary to determine how well the individual is doing her job. Being able to articulate the specifics of what you expect is critical to achieving results through others.

Setting objectives is the beginning of this continuous process of performance management. The ongoing conversations and meetings, at least quarterly, discussing progress on the expectations and identifying what support is needed for successful achievement of objectives is the middle. The final appraisal is the end. How can you possibly keep track of everything your direct report is doing? The answer is by keeping records.

Keeping Records

For most companies, there is a file kept by the personnel or human resources department for each employee. The manager needs to keep a different type of personnel file. The manager's file should include all information for an individual that affects his performance evaluations. This information includes the following:

❑ Documentation of all conversations regarding performance
❑ Written recordings of comments from customers (internal or external) about the individual's performance
❑ Documentation of observations you have made of the individual
❑ Letters of commendation
❑ E-mailed comments on performance or work
❑ Comments from your manager about the individual and/ or his work

What Other Records Do You Keep?

_____

_____

_____

_____

_____

_____

A Recommended File Structure

There are many different filing systems being used by managers for the purpose of collecting performance information on their direct reports. Certainly you may already have a method. Some managers use computer files, others use paper files. You may choose to use the format offered in the example provided in this book. Whichever method you use, be sure to keep it in a safe and secured location so that access to it is limited.

One example of a performance management file follows.

Informal Performance Discussions

Date	Topic and Comments	Initials

All Formal (Quarterly) Performance Discussion Documents

Date Sched	Date Held	Activity & Comments	Included in file ($\sqrt{}$)
		Objectives set	
		1st quarter review	
		2nd quarter review	
		3rd quarter review	
		Final review	
		Appraisal and rating	

Include copies of all documentation behind this page

Verbal Comments from Others Regarding the Performance of This Direct Report

Date	Topic and Comments	Initials

Letters or E-Mails for This Direct Report

Date	From	Topic and Comments

Include copies of all documentation behind this page

Next Steps to Performance Management

Later in the book, we will explore the three critical skills necessary for effectively developing and managing the performance of your direct reports: motivating, delegating, and coaching. Being able to use all of these skills is the key to individual development of your direct reports.

Action Planning Notes

Again, remember that to achieve success with your perform-ance as a manager and to have a successful team, it is important to take the time to consider what actions you will take at work. This will become the foundation for the final activity in this book.

Some examples are:

❏ Review each direct report's objectives with him to ensure they are SMART.

❏ Calendar quarterly performance discussions for each di-rect report.

What specific steps will you take with each of your direct reports to ensure that they have a clear understanding and com-mitment to the objectives that have been set? Also identify when you will have your next performance review session with each of them.

Individual	Action

CHAPTER 4

The Four Phases of Learning

As we move forward in improving our managerial skills, the next step to take is that of identifying what types of information and support each of our direct reports needs from us to be successful. One model to use in this determination is called the Four Phases of Learning Model. Using this model, we will investigate the following:

❏ Understanding what must be considered in evaluating the ability of our direct reports
❏ Determining in what phase of the Four Phases of Learning each individual is for each work task assigned
❏ Knowing how to interact with each person to achieve the greatest results

The Four Phases of Learning Model

This learning model is based on the assumption that every person approaches a specific work task with both a level of knowledge about how to do the work and a level of enthusiasm for that specific work. These levels can be anywhere from none to high. An individual can experience any combination of these two elements for any particular task.

The model supports the process of an individual moving forward through the phases of learning as her experience with the task progresses. Additional assumptions used in the model are that employees can and want to master their assigned work and that they can and want to do it with some degree of enthusiasm.

Given these assumptions and beliefs the model identifies Four Phases of Learning that an individual will go through when learning a new task. As a manager, you will need to identify where in that learning process each individual is on any given task.

Using the Model to Manage Direct Reports

We are all learning continuously. As we learned in Chapter 1, the very nature of our work environments is that they change regularly. Many of the changes affect the work that we ask our direct reports to do—the technology they use or support; their customer (internal or external) needs, wants, and expectations; the processes they follow; the needs of the company; as well as many other internal and external factors.

With all these changes, we too often unconsciously assume that our direct reports are at a particular level of expertise for all their assignments including new assignments we ask them to take. Without considering their expertise for each particular task, we usually manage them as we always have. Unfortunately, this usually leads us to overmanage or undermanage them. That is to say, we may give them too much information or support for the work (overmanaging), or we may give them too little information or support (undermanaging).

When we take the time to analyze how knowledgeable and enthusiastic each individual is for each task, project, or assignment, we can provide the correct amount of management. We must also remember that different people will begin at Phase 1 for a task while others, because of their knowledge and experience, may begin that same task at Phase 3.

Making Sense of the Four Phases

1. *Unknowing Incompetence.* Little knowledge about how to do the work, but a great amount of enthusiasm for doing it. This often occurs when someone is new to a task and they are very excited about the work, but don't have a good grasp of what is involved or required.
2. *Knowing Incompetence.* Growing knowledge, but still not too much. At this step, people have discovered what they must do, and often realize they are overwhelmed with the work. Their enthusiasm decreases with this realization.
3. *Knowing Competence.* Great knowledge, with room to improve and wavering enthusiasm. At this step, people have to think hard about what they are doing, and consequently have enthusiasm that changes from high to low.
4. *Unknowing Competence.* Great knowledge and great enthusiasm. The individual knows how to do the work and loves doing it and doesn't have to think about how to do it.

Activity: How Did You Feel?

In order to really understand what people experience while in the learning process, it is helpful to remember a time when you were learning to do something. It could be learning something personal, like a sport or musical instrument or foreign language, or learning something on the job. The Four Phases of Learning Model applies equally well.

We'll use your promotion to management for this activity.

1. Do you recall what you felt when you were promoted to manager? What was the feeling you experienced? Describe that feeling on the next page:

_____

_____

_____

_____

(It was probably one of enthusiasm and excitement. You weren't quite sure what all was required, but you knew you wanted the job.)

2. What happened next after reality set in? Describe that feeling here:

_____

_____

_____

_____

(It might have been disappointment or sadness that the job wasn't what you expected.)

3. Eventually we reach the third step where we have learned the basics but still have to work at it and can become discouraged. You may be at this step as you read this book, looking for guidance that will help you become more expert at your management responsibilities. Describe that feeling here:

_____

_____

_____

_____

(You probably love the job sometimes and are really frustrated by it other times.)

4. Thinking of a managerial skill you have mastered, consider how you feel about that aspect of managing. You no longer have to think about the work. You enjoy that aspect of your job because you do it well. Describe that feeling here:

_____

_____

_____

_____

(Happiness is the usual feeling at this step.)

A Model Description

As you consider the feelings that you have experienced, you can understand what other people experience. One way to look at these phases follows in Figure 4-1.

Figure 4-1. Knowledge and enthusiasm.

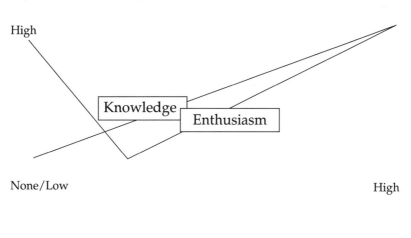

It is every manager's dream to have all of his or her direct reports at the unknowing competence (Phase 4) level for all the work they do. When this happens, the manager can delegate work and know that it will be completed in the manner desired. And every manager, by using the phases of learning, can make this happen. Let's look at how you manage your direct reports using this model.

Identifying the Phases of Learning

The first step in managing people using the phases of learning is to identify what phase they are in for the particular task you are asking them to do. Doing that correctly requires that you ask yourself and/or your direct reports several questions:

❑ Do you want to do this work?
❑ How comfortable are you with the specific task?
❑ What have you done before that is similar to this work?
❑ How will you approach this task?

What other questions would you ask to determine enthusiasm and knowledge for the work you have asked your direct reports to do?

_____

_____

_____

_____

_____

_____

_____

_____

_____

_____

_____

Looking at the individual tasks for each person, you can follow these guidelines for actions to take to ensure you are not overmanaging or undermanaging your direct reports.

Phase	Knowledge	Enthusiasm	Management Action
1. Unknowing Incompetence	Little	Great	Provide structure, direction, information, training, supervision
2. Knowing Incompetence	Little, Some	Little	Provide some structure, direction, information, allow input, motivation, encouragement, support
3. Knowing Competence	Great, Some	Up and Down	Provide motivation, encouragement, major input
4. Unknowing Competence	Great	Great	Provide goals, express confidence

As identified in the preceding chart, people need different actions from their managers depending on what learning phase they are in for each specific task. Here are some actions you can take once you have identified the phase:

Managing the Unknowing Incompetence Phase

❑ People are doing something for the first time. They may have some applicable experience they can use.

❑ They are eager to get started.

❑ They need SMART objectives, clear procedures, close supervision and training.

❑ They may not be able to contribute many ideas to the plan.

❑ The manager helps them to build new skills as they try to reach objectives.

Managing the Knowing Incompetence Phase

❑ The person realizes how difficult the task is and how much will be involved in accomplishing it.

❑ The manager needs to encourage the individual to continue his efforts.

❑ The individual still needs SMART objectives, clear procedures, and possibly more training.

❑ The person needs information about what he is doing well and what he may need to do differently.

❑ The person needs opportunities to offer input to the work requirements and outputs.

Managing the Knowing Competence Phase

❑ The person realizes she can do the task, but she needs to work hard and think about doing it.

❑ The manager needs to encourage the individual to continue her efforts.

❑ The person needs information about what she is doing well.

❑ The person needs opportunities to offer input to the work requirements and outputs.

Managing the Unknowing Competence Phase

❏ The person now can do the job without much concern and wants to do the job.

❏ The manager needs to provide the goals.

❏ The person still needs SMART objectives.

❏ The manager needs to express confidence in the person's work.

Pinpointing the Phases

Now that you know what to look for and how to respond to what you find, review the following cases to determine in which phase of the Four Phases of Learning each individual is for the task he is asked to do. List the manager's actions in response to the phase.

CASE A

Andrew, who completed his master's degree recently, has joined your team. He has excellent academic credentials, better than most other team members. You have assigned him to maintenance work on existing production programs. After two weeks on the job, he comes to you and says: "I've decided to quit. I thought I would like programming but this is tedious. I can't follow the logic of the modules and I don't think they were well-written. Mary in the next cubicle only has an associate's degree and she is working on new Internet development, while I'm stuck on the out-of-date applications. The prescribed maintenance process is too laborious. I don't know why I have to follow it."

❏ Andrew's phase of learning:

❏ Manager's action:

CASE B

Alison has been working at the help desk for six months. She volunteered for the assignment and had the right people and technical skills. She was doing great until recently. She has been coming in late, not returning calls promptly, and missing important deadlines. You just got a call from the vice president of marketing who was angry that Alison did not get his new Prospect Tracking functioning on his Palm computer. He made several calls and she was slow to respond. She didn't seem to care that it was impacting his ability to lead his division.

❑ Alison's phase of learning:

❑ Manager's action:

CASE C

Juan has been project lead on several small projects and always does a good job. He has a knack for keeping things on track and juggling several things at once. The projects have not involved supervising people, although several required him to work with peers. He got along well and is a friendly sociable person. He has asked you for a larger project that requires leading a team. He took the company's project management course and wants to apply his knowledge and use the new project management software.

❑ Juan's phase of learning:

❑ Manager's action:

CASE D

Mei Ling joined your team recently as a senior chemist. She has an impressive résumé and has published several papers on anomalies in polymer chemistry, which first brought her to your attention. You have just been asked to set up a new polymer research project to investigate breakthrough solutions for product development. Mei Ling has directed large research projects and seems to be able to get chemists accustomed to working auton-omously to work as a team.

❑ Mei Ling's phase of learning:

❑ Manager's action:

CASE E

Pat was assigned to the technical training team three months ago. He is recognized as a technical expert in developing and installing complex net-works on multiple platforms in remote sites. Pat brings a depth of knowledge to every class, and the overall seminar evaluation scores have been im-proving steadily. Pat had difficulty with the "clear explanations" and "classroom management" cate-gories but has improved with tutoring. You are sat-isfied with Pat's progress.

Pat has just come into your office. "I'm concerned about this training assignment. I'm working too hard. I spent seventy-three hours preparing for a two-day class. If I keep up this pace, I'll burn out fast. I have to plan everything in great detail. Peo-ple ask me questions and when I don't know the answer, I don't like it. My ratings are improving, but how long will it be before I get great ones?"

❑ Pat's phase of learning:

❑ Manager's action:

THE ANSWERS

Case A. Andrew is at Phase 2, Knowing Incompe-tence. His manager needs to take the following actions: Provide some structure, direction, and in-formation about how to do the job. The manager needs to allow Andrew to provide some input to the work, and to create opportunities for Andrew to be successful to increase his motivation. His manager needs to encourage Andrew and provide support for his effort.

Case B. Alison is at Phase 3, Knowing Competence. Her manager needs to spend time focusing on Alison's efforts and successes. He also needs to provide recognition to create a motivating environment, including encouraging Alison to provide input to the work. He doesn't need to tell her how to do the work.

Case C. Juan is at Phase 1, Unknowing Incompetence. His manager needs to give him a lot of direction on how to do the job. He needs structure, information, training, and close supervision.

Case D. Mei Ling is at Phase 4, Unknowing Competence. Her manager needs to define the roles each will take, and express confidence in Mei Ling's work.

Case E. Pat is at Phase 3, Knowing Competence. His manager needs to tell him how well he is doing based on the improved seminar evaluation scores and to let him know that it is all right not to know all the answers. He needs to be asked what he thinks will improve his ratings.

Your Own Applications

Select two of the people with whom you work. Each person should be someone to whom you will delegate a significant work assignment. Answer the following questions:

Person #1:
❑ Where is this person in the Four Phases of Learning for this task?
❑ What are the behaviors of this person that make you assign this phase?

Referring to the Four Phases of Learning, note the general approaches recommended for managers in the management action column. Given the tasks this person needs to do and the facts in this situation, describe in specific terms the actions you should take to follow the general guidelines for managing this employee, given her or his phase of learning.

Person #2
❑ Where is this person in the Four Phases of Learning for this task?
❑ What are the behaviors of this person that make you assign this phase?

Referring to the Four Phases of Learning, note the general approaches recommended for managers in the management action column. Given the tasks this person needs to do and the facts in this situation, describe in specific terms the actions you should take to follow the general guidelines for managing this employee, given her or his phase of learning.

Guidelines for Managing Direct Reports in the Four Phases of Learning

❑ Assess each person's phase of learning for each task, project, or assignment.
❑ Provide the appropriate level of information, input, and encouragement.
❑ Watch for signs that the person is entering a new phase and adjust your activity accordingly.
❑ Remember, people can be in different phases for different assignments.
❑ Use delegation, motivation, and coaching to manage each phase.

Action Planning Notes

Remember, in order to achieve success with your performance as a manager and to have a successful team, it is important to take the time to consider what actions you will take at work. This will become the foundation for the final activity in this book.

Some examples are:
❑ Identify the learning phase for each task for each direct report.
❑ Determine what support and direction are needed for success.

Identify the development level for some tasks for each of your staff members. What will you change about your interactions with them to help them be successful?

Individual	Action

CHAPTER 5

Motivation

In addition to understanding where each of your direct reports is in the Four Phases of Learning for each of his or her responsibilities, it helps to understand what motivates that person to work. In order to know what that is, it is necessary to understand the underlying theories of motivation and then look at how you can apply that information to your real situations. In this chapter, we will:

❑ Apply the classic motivation model of Frederick Herzberg
❑ Identify the causes of dissatisfaction in your workplace
❑ Uncover your employees' motivations
❑ Capitalize on your employees' natural motivators for success

How to Motivate a Direct Report

A great many managers view motivation as a polite word for describing what they perceive as their authority or power position. "Whether or not you like it, I'm going to get you to do what I want you to do." This kind of *motivation* is extrinsic, that is, it is external. When this type of motivation is applied, people feel like there is hammer being held to their heads. Many of these extrinsic motivators are perceived as a threat to the individual. We may get results in the short term, but the long-term impact of that approach to motivating direct reports leads to resentment, hostility, and demotivation.

The only motivation that truly works is intrinsic or self-motivation. We cannot force someone else to be motivated. What we can provide is an environment in which an individual can become motivated. In order to provide this environment, we need to understand what creates motivation in others.

Where Motivation Originates

Frederick Herzberg, a behavioral scientist and author of *The Motivation to Work,* developed a motivation theory specifically for the workplace that he termed the Motivator-Hygiene Theory. This theory, based on the earlier work of Abraham Maslow, is divided into two factors. As you review the elements in this theory, remember that different things motivate different people, and that there are very different motivators for people of different ages with different life experiences. For instance, casual dress may be more attractive to people who are accustomed to wearing casual clothing (for example, recent students) than to people who have been in the workforce and have already invested in a business wardrobe.

The Two-Factor Theory

Herzberg's Motivator-Hygiene Theory stresses that some job factors lead to satisfaction while others can only prevent dissatisfaction.

Hygiene Factors

Herzberg argues that there are elements in the workplace that must be present in order for motivation to exist. He refers to these elements as hygiene or maintenance factors.

Hygiene or maintenance factors include:

❑ *Pay*. Salaries or wages must be equivalent to those in the same industry in the same geographic area.
❑ *Status*. People's status within the company, typically identified with titles, must be recognized and maintained.
❑ *Security*. Your direct reports must feel that their jobs are as secure as can be in the current work environment.
❑ *Working Conditions*. The workplace must be clean, have windows, or other environmental elements that are typical for the industry.
❑ *Fringe Benefits*. Health care, elder care, day care, employee assistance programs, and other typical benefits must be offered.
❑ *Policies and Administrative Practices*. These include flex hours, vacation schedules, dress codes, scheduling, and other practices that affect workers.
❑ *Interpersonal Relations*. There must be acceptable levels of interpersonal contact including the absence of threats, ongoing conflict, humiliation, and so forth.

Herzberg stated that, in a work environment, these hygiene factors relate to the context of a job and will tend to eliminate job dissatisfaction if present in proper form for the individual. Though their presence can create short-term job satisfaction and help maintain the organization, these factors will not necessarily motivate staff.

For instance, allowing casual dress may satisfy them initially. After a short while, though, such conditions will be taken for granted. Maintenance factors are not capable of producing strong long-term satisfaction or motivation. Changing back to standard business dress, on the other hand, may cause employee dissatisfaction and eventually reduce motivation.

Motivational Factors

Because of Herzberg's belief that hygiene factors are not motivators, he concentrated on what managers can do to address the needs of an individual related to his achievement of his own self-esteem and confidence.

❑ *Achievement.* Work must provide the opportunity for individuals to gain a sense of achievement. The job must have a beginning and an end, and have a product of some sort.
❑ *Responsibility.* In order for the achievement to be felt, the individual must feel responsible for the work.
❑ *Meaningfulness.* The work itself must be meaningful to the individual in order to promote motivation.
❑ *Recognition.* This motivator should be used extensively to ensure that direct reports know their managers are aware of their accomplishments.
❑ *Opportunities for Growth and Advancement.* These opportunities must exist for the individual to be motivated.

Looking at Your Workplace and Addressing the Maintenance Factors

Herzberg's work suggests a two-stage process for managing employee satisfaction and motivation.

First, managers should address maintenance factors, so that basic needs are met and employees do not become dissatisfied. Managers must ensure that employees are adequately paid, working conditions are safe and clean, workers have opportunities for social interaction, and treatment by managers is fair and humane.

These maintenance factors have changed as the workplace has changed. In days past, having an interesting job for which there were adequate compensation and reasonable working conditions was good enough. However, as the workplace has expanded to include many different generations with different life experiences and expectations, the elements of work that can cause dissatisfaction have changed.

Today, maintenance factors such as benefits, vacation time, work location, work scheduling and hours, and environment should be looked at, so that the employees do not become dissatisfied.

In some cases, these factors are not under your managerial control. Many times, they are negotiated by parties outside of your immediate work group.

What Are the Dissatisfiers in Your Workplace?

_____

_____

_____

_____

_____

_____

_____

What You Can Do

Although you may not be able to actually change the issue that is causing your direct report's dissatisfaction, it is important that this dissatisfaction be addressed. If the dissatisfaction is ignored, it will inhibit the progress of motivation or performance improvement.

You must, therefore, work through the dissatisfaction issues to the best of your ability. The following are suggestions for working through the issues that surface:

❑ *Acknowledge the situation.* In some instances, paying attention, acknowledging the situation, and discussing it can satisfy a direct report. The fact that you have put the issue out on the table and are willing to hear the person's concerns can be enough to minimize, and sometimes eliminate, the dissatisfaction.

❑ *Communicate.* Many times, employees are not aware of why a policy needs to be changed or office space reduced. The manager must be available for questions and explanations. Explaining why a situation has occurred and discussing it with staff provides understanding and often alleviates dissatisfaction.

❑ *Work toward a solution.* Meeting with a direct report and jointly charting a course are important actions. Beyond acknowledging a situation, discussing a plan to move toward resolving the issue (if feasible) may be required to minimize or eliminate dissatisfaction.

❑ *Take action.* Sometimes taking action and getting results are the only ways to satisfy a direct report. If action is not a realistic option, you must communicate that fact.

Motivational Factors

The second stage for managing the satisfaction and motivation of your direct reports is addressing the motivators— ensuring that your staff members experience the internal motivators that drive them to success.

Because these natural motivators are internal and subjective, what is naturally motivating to one person may be different for another. These motivators are tied to job outcomes or the tasks associated with the work environment.

Remember:
What Motivates You May *Not* Motivate Others

Looking at the motivators listed previously more closely, we can see that there are some specific issues that may impact the motivation level of our individual direct reports. This is a good checklist for evaluating what might be missing from the work of our direct reports.

Achievement

❑ Is there an opportunity for a sense of completion?
❑ Are there goals and targets to which individuals can relate?
❑ Is there a sense of ownership?
❑ Is there a plan in place for ongoing feedback?
❑ Can the person measure any progress in attaining goals?
❑ Does this job require a person to learn more or to develop more technical knowledge and expertise?

Responsibility

❑ Is there a degree of freedom in the job?
❑ Is the person in control of her own behavior?
❑ Is there a degree of risk involved?
❑ Does the individual have the authority to make decisions and solve problems on her own?
❑ Does she direct the work of others?
❑ Is she accountable for important resources?

Recognition

❑ Is there an opportunity for visibility?
❑ Is there an opportunity for recognition by management?
❑ Do accomplishments get noticed or publicized?
❑ Is performing this job a preparation for higher levels of responsibility?
❑ Is it good training for moving laterally?

Meaningfulness

❑ Is it challenging?
❑ Does the work have value in and of itself?
❑ Does it allow him personal growth?
❑ Does it increase his self-confidence?
❑ Does it improve his ability to work with others?

Opportunities for Growth and Advancement

❑ Can employees learn from their work?
❑ Is promotion (lateral or vertical) possible?

❑ Can employees learn new skills?
❑ Will others in the organization see the results of the employee's work?

What Actions Can You Take with Your Work Group to Increase the Opportunity for Motivation?

_____

_____

_____

_____

_____

_____

_____

_____

_____

_____

Identifying Motivating Factors in Individuals

In order to respond to the needs of your direct reports, you must first be able to identify what their needs are. One way of learning this information is to *observe the direct report's actions.* Another way is to simply *ask the direct report what motivates him.* Remember that asking questions in a supportive way shows that you care about the individual and want to use the information you learn in positive ways.

Because we tend to think that people are just like us, it is important to recall that not everyone is motivated by the same things or to the same degree. It is critical that you listen to what your staff members are saying and carefully observe what they are doing.

Once the factors are identified, take action to address them. Work with others, if necessary, to determine what changes can be made to increase motivation. Provide the environment, the direction, and support for the given situation, and the motivation will come on its own. Remember the premise behind the Four Phases of Learning Model is that people can and want to develop. Motivation is a key performance management concept because by creating a motivational environment, you help to improve your employees' performance. Providing them with the right environment and the right amount of direction and support will increase their competence and commitment, which is their motivation, and gives them the enthusiasm and confidence to achieve success at work.

Capitalizing on Your Direct Report's Motivation

As you plan the actions you can take in your work environment, consider instituting the following motivators in your organization:

Satisfying the Achievement Need
❑ Ensure that goals are set and monitored on an ongoing basis.
❑ Provide ongoing feedback on goal achievement.
❑ If goals are in jeopardy, discuss them with your direct report and provide support and suggestions to ensure that goals are met.
❑ When people resist taking on a new job, make sure you

build in learning time and success factors. Individuals who fear failure will resist new jobs.

❑ Offer training opportunities, either in-house or from an outside source.

❑ Offer your direct report the opportunity to team up with someone else to learn a new skill.

Satisfying Responsibility Needs

❑ Provide opportunities for your direct report to be visible and/or to wield influence.

❑ Ask for advice, opinions, and suggestions.

❑ Delegate, that is, provide opportunities for your direct report to organize and direct an activity.

Satisfying Recognition Needs

❑ Provide opportunities for a direct report to work with others when possible.

❑ Provide opportunities for the direct report to be visible.

❑ Establish a relationship that provides feedback and attention.

Satisfying Meaningfulness Needs

❑ Offer the employee an opportunity to cross-train.

❑ Give the direct report a chance to take on a new responsibility as part of his duties.

❑ Ask the employee what would make work more meaningful.

Satisfying Growth and Opportunity Needs

❑ Ask the employee about her career objectives.

❑ Find cross-training and rotational opportunities for the employee.

❑ Provide training opportunities to the employee on a subject she wants to learn.

Putting a Plan into Place—Capitalizing on Your Direct Report's Motivation

Now that you have some specific ideas of what to consider, think of an individual in your organization who has been a challenge: low in productivity, absent, or upset. Based on what you have learned, develop a plan to address the motivation of that person.

1. Using the list that follows, identify what motivates this individual. List the instances that validate your perception.

   Achievement:

   _____

   _____

   Responsibility:

   _____

   _____

   Meaningfulness:

   _____

   _____

   Recognition:

   _____

   _____

Opportunities for Growth and Advancement:

_____

_____

2. Determine what you can implement to motivate this person and keep him motivated.

_____

_____

_____

_____

_____

_____

_____

_____

_____

_____

_____

_____

Motivation Summary

Key points to remember as you implement a plan to improve your motivational environments are:

❑ Everyone is motivated differently.
❑ There will be a mix of motivational factors among your direct reports. Some people are motivated by meaningfulness while others are motivated by recognition.
❑ As a manager, you must also focus on your motivation—because if you are not motivated, you cannot motivate others.
❑ Walk the talk. Act motivated and your direct reports will model your behavior.
❑ As a manager, you need to recognize that your direct reports' motivational factors may be different than your own. It is your responsibility, in spite of the differences, to do whatever it takes to provide opportunities and assignments for your direct reports that will tap into their personal motivational factors whenever possible.
❑ The bottom line is that you, as a manager, are responsible for getting your direct reports to perform, and that creating the right environment will ensure that they will do what you need them to do.

Motivating with Coaching and Delegating

Providing your direct reports the right environment with the right amount of direction and support will increase the potential for having motivated individuals on your team. In the next two chapters, we will explore ways to delegate and coach your direct reports to enable them to grow in their knowledge and consequently their enthusiasm for the work they do for your organization. All of these factors strongly influence their motivation.

Action Planning Notes

In order to achieve success with your performance as a manager and to have a successful team, it is important to take the time to consider what actions you will take at work. Remember to be specific. This will become the foundation for the final activity in this book.

Some examples are:

❑ Determine primary motivational factors for all your direct reports by observing them or through discussions with them.

❑ Break down production of the annual data report into smaller components (for those who are motivated by achievement).

What can you do to improve motivation for each of your direct reports?

Individual	Action

CHAPTER 6

Delegation for Growth and Development

As you master the managerial skills of the identification of the learning phases and learn what motivates each of your direct reports, you can begin the process of evaluating the work for which you have responsibility and determine what you can delegate and what work you must do yourself. Delegation is, perhaps, the single most difficult skill for new managers to acquire. To learn how to develop that skill, we will:

❑ Explore the importance of delegation as a key performance management skill
❑ Identify the benefits of delegating
❑ Assess your own comfort with delegating
❑ Learn the steps to take for delegation success
❑ Practice making delegation assignments

Delegation: What Is It Really?

Webster's dictionary says delegation is "to entrust to another." As managers entrust to another, typically their direct reports, they create opportunities for these individuals to enhance their knowledge and/or skill level for specific tasks. Delegation allows another individual or group to work on a project or task that offers motivation and rewards on its successful completion. It also offers the manager the opportunity to grow and develop individuals who can then be recognized as high-level contributors in the organization. Effective delegation can be accomplished by coaching employees to improve their skills and knowledge level. Coaching will be covered in Chapter 7.

Managers who delegate effectively have direct reports who are more capable and enthusiastic because of their delegation experience. The direct reports are seen as competent and committed to take on more projects or tasks, thereby freeing up the manager's time to work on tasks that cannot be delegated.

As valuable a management skill as it is, too often delegation is either nonexistent or done half-heartedly or haphazardly. When the delegation is done half-heartedly, people become dissatisfied and demotivated, and they will not improve their skill or knowledge levels.

Delegation is another key performance management tool because it will help you to improve the performance of your work groups, your organization, and your management skills. A good manager knows that delegation is the way to *achieve results through others.*

The Benefits

Why should you as a manager want to delegate some of your work? After all, won't that make others think that you are not able to do everything for which you have responsibility? Absolutely not.

Remember:
The Manager's Job Is to Accomplish Work
Through and With Others

Until you involve others, you will probably struggle with your role as a manager. You will feel like you have more tasks than time to do them. You may feel overwhelmed by the workload and responsibilities. You may hate coming in to work because facing the day is so difficult. You may even begin to have stress-related illnesses or relationship problems.

In addition to the many personal reasons to learn to delegate, there are also many business reasons to learn to delegate. These reasons may include but are not limited to:

❑ More work can be accomplished
❑ Direct reports become more involved
❑ Helps you manage your workload
❑ Remote locations can be more effectively managed
❑ Development of direct reports
❑ Builds a high-performance team
❑ Draws upon the strengths of the entire organization
❑ Work is done at the lowest cost possible
❑ Reduces your stress

List Other Reasons:

_____

_____

_____

_____

_____

When a manager delegates, it is a demonstration of:

❑ Self-confidence (not afraid that others will show you up)
❑ Confidence in your direct reports
❑ Value for and support of individual development
❑ Commitment to success of the organization (rather than being focused on own agenda)

One final reason to delegate is that it gives you more time and energy to focus on activities that are more important to the company as well as personally developmental—which move your own career forward.

If you continue to do the work that someone who reports to you can do, then you are:

❑ Wasting your time
❑ Losing a development opportunity
❑ Weakening the entire organization
❑ Not performing your role as a manager

Steven R. Covey states in *The Seven Habits of Highly Effective People* that "effectively delegating to others is perhaps the single most powerful high-leverage activity there is."[1] And yet, in spite of that reason, it is often avoided or misused. Delegation tends to not happen at all, or it is done randomly and without much thought or planning. And when it is done badly, it can be more harmful than productive.

Managers Who Delegate Effectively Have Direct Reports Who Are More Capable and Enthusiastic

The Barriers

If delegation is such a powerful tool and we recognize the benefits, what keeps us from delegating? Despite its obvious advantages, few managers, particularly new managers, delegate. We each have our own reasons. Here are a few common objections to delegation:

❑ Preference for doing the work oneself. "Why should I delegate a task I like to do, or one that I do so well?"

❑ Concern that the delegate will not complete the task as well as you. "I can do it better myself."

❑ Lack of experience in delegating. "I don't know how to go about starting."

❑ I'm supposed to have all the answers. "People will think I don't know how to do it."

List Other Reasons:

_____

_____

_____

_____

_____

Even Experienced Managers Hesitate to Delegate

It is critical that you overcome the barriers to delegating because the benefits far outweigh the barriers. Remember, it is your role as a manager to develop your direct reports so that organizational goals can be accomplished. You really can't afford not to delegate. And when you become an effective delegator, you will have the ability to leave an important legacy as a manager.

A Successful Manager's Legacy:
Confident, Competent People Who Are Committed
to Personal Excellence and Organizational Success

Quiz: What Is My Comfort Level with Delegation?

When I am overloaded with work, I look to my direct reports to take on some of my work.

Always	Usually	Sometimes	Never
❑	❑	❑	❑

I let my direct reports know what I expect of them.

Always	Usually	Sometimes	Never
❑	❑	❑	❑

After I have delegated a project, all of my team members know who is leading the project and his level of authority on the project.

Always	Usually	Sometimes	Never
❑	❑	❑	❑

When I delegate work to any of my direct reports, I provide him with all the information I have on the subject.

Always	Usually	Sometimes	Never
❑	❑	❑	❑

In my organization, delegation is perceived as an opportunity for growth and recognition.

Always	Usually	Sometimes	Never
❑	❑	❑	❑

I consider the skills and knowledge of my direct reports before assigning them a project.

Always	Usually	Sometimes	Never
❑	❑	❑	❑

I stress the results I am looking for, not how to achieve them, when I assign work to my direct reports.

Always	Usually	Sometimes	Never
❑	❑	❑	❑

It is easy for me to delegate work to qualified employees.

Always	Usually	Sometimes	Never
❑	❑	❑	❑

After delegating work, I stay in touch with my direct report on the progress being made.

Always	Usually	Sometimes	Never
❑	❑	❑	❑

I hold the assigned direct report responsible for the results of the work.

Always	Usually	Sometimes	Never
❑	❑	❑	❑

The more you answered "always" to the above statements, the more effective you are at delegating.

What Tasks Can Be Delegated?

Clearly, delegation takes practice, and knowing what kinds of tasks can be delegated is the first step in this process. You must realize that not all tasks can be delegated, despite the abilities of your direct reports. The first step to delegation is to decide what to delegate.

Tasks that can effectively be given to others include:

❑ Tasks closely related to the work employees are already doing
❑ Tasks with clearly defined procedures and end results
❑ Repetitive tasks that fit into the normal work flow
❑ Tasks that enable employees to develop themselves
❑ Routine and necessary tasks including detail work and information gathering
❑ Work where others are more qualified, such as proofing, research, and specialized technical work

When you are thinking of tasks, projects, and responsibilities to delegate, a question you may ask yourself is:

Is this something someone else could do?

If the answer if yes, then *delegate* it.

In some cases, delegation is not appropriate. These cases include but are not limited to:

❏ Tasks not clearly defined, or about which uncertainty exists
❏ Really important tasks that management expects the manager to handle
❏ Serious understaffing—delegating could overwhelm direct reports
❏ Long-term planning and goals
❏ Key decisions
❏ Crisis situations
❏ Personnel matters including salary, discipline, and other confidential activities
❏ Personal assignments

It is important to realize that not everything can or should be delegated; however, every new manager needs to watch for opportunities to delegate and do so every time he possibly can.

Activity: What Should I Delegate?

The first step in delegation is to identify all the activities you typically do in a week or month. Without this first step, choices about what to delegate can't be made. List as many of your activities/tasks/responsibilities as you can. Then place them into three categories: (1) Eliminate, (2) Delegate, (3) Keep and prioritize. This will give you a list of delegation opportunities on which you can act immediately.

Activity	Eliminate	Delegate	Keep and Prioritize
1.			
2.			
3.			
4.			
5.			
6.			
7.			
8.			
9.			
10.			

Delegating at All Ability Levels

As a manager, you can delegate to your direct reports regardless of their current ability to do the work, as long as you take the time and effort to teach them. Many assignments can be delegated in pieces—that is, break down the larger task and assign a portion of the work to an individual. As that individual develops her skills at this assignment, additional components of the larger task can be delegated. This would be considered progressive delegation, starting with more manager involvement and working toward complete task delegation.

Making Delegation Successful

When you realize that you should be delegating, and you are comfortable with what tasks, projects, or responsibilities you can delegate, how do you go about it? There are some specific steps that you can follow that will help to ensure your success.

1. Analyze the Specific Task That Needs to Be Done
❑ What is the scope of the work?
❑ How important or visible is the outcome?
❑ When does it need to be done? Is it urgent or is there time to train someone?
❑ What are the specific measurable goals?
❑ What is the level of responsibility you are delegating?
❑ What resources (tools, budgets, people, and other resources) are available?

Once you have a clear understanding of the task, you are ready to move on to the next step. In order to take this next step, you must know your people—their skills, experience, and knowledge. What you don't know about them you need to find out, and the best source of information is the individual himself. What information can you find out about your direct reports that would help you to decide if they are the right match for the job/activity you want to delegate? The following list may help you determine what to look for:

❑ Areas of strength/weakness
❑ Capabilities
❑ Developmental needs
❑ Past work experience
❑ Career aspirations
❑ Fears and/or concerns

If you don't know this about each of your direct reports, you can get the information by asking each one about previous experience, goals, and career aspirations, and what he or she knows. You can also review personnel files for their past experience, and you can talk to their former bosses. Once you have the necessary information, you can proceed to step two.

2. Identify the Best Direct Report for the Job
❑ What skills and experience do you need?
❑ Whom do you have on your staff that can meet those needs?
❑ Is there time on the delegated task to use this as a developmental activity?
❑ What training and/or support will the individual need to be successful?

3. Meet with the Person and Explain What You Need Done
❑ Describe the task and the goals.
❑ Specify why this person has been selected.
❑ Be specific about responsibilities and authority.
❑ Get the person's agreement that she will take this assignment.

4. Implement the Delegation
❑ Share the individual's information of the assignment with other staff members.

❑ Allow the individual to "run with the project"—don't interfere unnecessarily.
❑ Establish a follow-up plan.

5. Hold the Follow-Up Meetings
❑ Make yourself available for support.
❑ Discover problems early.
❑ Determine what you will need to do to ensure success.
❑ Praise what has been done well, and redirect what could have been done better.

As you proceed through these steps, keep in mind that delegation is a process, not an event. Keep the following in mind:

❑ Make the entire delegation process as collaborative as possible.
❑ Keep the lines of communication open.
❑ Tailor your monitoring to the individual.
❑ Ask for regular progress reports (frequency depending on the individual).
❑ Take periodic samplings of their work.
❑ Provide timely feedback.
❑ Encourage solution thinking.
❑ Recognize that mistakes are part of learning. (How can you do it differently/more effectively next time?)
❑ Celebrate successes (even small ones).

As you begin to delegate, you must remember that it is important to select the right person for the assignment. You will need to be prepared to work with that person on developing the new skills necessary for effective completion of the work. Use the Four Phases of Learning to determine if there is a match between the person and the assignment and work with the selected individual for your mutual success.

Delegation Assignments Activity

As you consider the steps to take, and the considerations to make, return to your list of delegation opportunities that you identified earlier and choose the four most urgent tasks to be completed. Thinking of your staff members, and the skills and experience of each one, complete the following delegation activity for one task. When you have completed the activity on the next page, you will be prepared to implement delegation with your direct reports, creating opportunities for all of them to be more motivated about the work they are doing.

Delegation Activity: Choose the "Right" Person

1. Task: _____

2. Degree of urgency: High   Med   Low
    Degree of importance: High   Med   Low

3. Outcomes Required:
    (1)

    (2)

    (3)

4. Choice of most competent person: _____
    Why?

5. Choice of the person for whom it could be developmental: _____
    Why?
    Does he have the basic skill set to produce the outcomes required? _____
    What kind of coaching/support would be needed? (Do I have the time to provide it?)

6. The right person for this assignment is: _____

7. His learning phase on this assignment is: _____

8. I will hold the delegation meeting on _____

Delegation Case Study

Now that you have learned the benefits and barriers to effective delegation and the steps and considerations to take when delegating, you will be able to evaluate situations such as the one that follows. Take the time to read through this case study and answer the questions at the end. This will reinforce your new knowledge on this subject.

CLEAR DIRECTIONS: AUGUST 1

The expense reimbursement process at your company recently changed from manual to electronic input. In the manual process, each employee was required to submit a handwritten form with the expenses listed on it. Employees were required to get approval from their managers prior to sending the form via company mail to the accounting department. Often their managers were traveling and the forms sat on their desks from several days to a week or longer. This process took several weeks for reimbursement of the employee by check.

The new electronic system was designed to make the reimbursement process go more smoothly and quickly: The employee submits expenses through a computer program, which automatically forwards the completed expense form to the manager via the company network. After reviewing the form, which the manager is required to complete within twenty-four hours of receiving it, she forwards it via the company network to the accounting department. The accounting department then has twenty-four to forty-eight hours to process the expense reimbursement and submit the money via electronic funds transfer to the employee's checking account.

There have been, however, strong objections to using this new process. Employees are complaining that they haven't had sufficient training for the new system and that it is cumbersome for them to use. In addition, there is some concern from the managers that they might not be able to review their e-mail on a daily basis while they are traveling.

Additionally, they are concerned that if there are questions about any of the expenses, there is no easy way to get the question answered by the employee before forwarding it to accounting. All in all, people are resisting using the new process and want to return to the old way.

Instructions need to be revised and more training needs to be provided to both the employees and their managers. The instructions need to be written and training sessions need to be scheduled, but not delivered, by August 10. The training sessions need to be delivered by the end of August.

Your staff of four is very competent, having four to ten years' experience with the company. One of your staff members, Jerry, is excellent at organizing tasks. He has been in his position for eight years and has the respect of other staff members. His only shortcoming is that he has not spent much time actually working with the new system.

Casey, another staff member, is good with details and seems to work well with others, but occasionally he is late completing his work. You have spoken to him about this, and he has promised to be more prompt. Casey has ten years' experience with the company and has held his current position for six years.

Pat has four years' experience in the organization. She has the most technical expertise about this system, and enjoys talking to others, one-on-one, about its operation. Her organizational skills are not yet fully developed, and she has a lack of confidence when addressing a group of people.

T.J. also has four years of experience in the organization. She has primarily been involved in the follow-up work with late payment concerns. Her involvement in the new system has been limited to what she has heard from others in your group.

You became their manager approximately one year ago when you came from outside the organization. You have a good relationship with all your direct reports, but right now have little time to spend with them on this subject.

What Are You Going to Do?

Considering the steps to delegation, answer the following questions:

1. Would you delegate? Why? Why not?

_____

_____

_____

2. What specifically would you delegate?

_____

_____

_____

3. To whom would you delegate? And how much of the situation would you delegate to that person?

_____

_____

_____

4. How would you go about delegating using the steps to delegation?

_____

_____

_____

Here are some possible answers:

1. Yes, I would delegate because staff has the ability to revise the instructions and they can schedule the training sessions.
2. I would delegate the revision of the instructions after my direct reports had investigated the specific problems and the scheduling of the training.
3. Give the overall assignment to Jerry for his organizational skills. Ask him to provide me with information on how he would use the entire staff to complete this assignment. (He may suggest that Pat would be best to assist with the technical information for the training, Casey would be best used in the writing of the instructions, and T.J. would be an excellent proofreader. If he doesn't suggest this, find out what his rationale is for his recommendations.)

Note

1. Covey, Stephen R., *The Seven Habits of Highly Effective People* (New York: Fireside Simon & Schuster, 1989).

Action Planning Notes

In order to achieve success with your performance as a manager and to have a successful team, it is important to take the time to consider what actions you will take at work. This will become the foundation for the final activity in this book.

Some examples are:
❑ Delegate the agenda for staff meetings.
❑ Delegate the data anlysis for the project to someone for whom it would be a growth assignment.

Identify one task that you will delegate to each of your direct reports. When will you delegate it?

Individual	Action

CHAPTER 7

Coaching for Performance

Once you have begun to delegate, you need to be able to work with your direct reports so that they are successful in their assignments. This managerial skill is referred to as *coaching*. Effective coaching will lead to your ultimate role of *achieving results through and with others*. In this chapter, we will:

❑ Explore the importance of coaching as a key performance management skill
❑ Uncover your strengths as a coach
❑ Describe techniques to improve performance effectively
❑ Plan a coaching session

Why Coach?

Simply put, you coach to enhance the development of skills and the performance of your direct reports. You cannot improve employee performance without coaching. Given these

115

reasons to coach, why is it more important now than it has ever been?

As stated in Chapter 1, companies have been going through revolutionary changes in the past few decades. Managers are now required to increase productivity with fewer resources than in previous years. Industries have developed in which the rate of change in product offerings happens at lightning speed—products that are not yet on the market are already outdated!

In order to meet the demands of the marketplace and company investors, managers must create a culture of continuous learning. The old "command and control" approach to managing direct reports has become ineffective. Managers must improve the performance of their direct reports through coaching and facilitating their growth and development.

What Is Coaching?

Coaching Is the Process of Creating the Environment and Building the Relationships That Enhance the Development of Skills and the Performance of Both the Direct Reports and the Manager

Typically, we think of coaching as an opportunity to improve someone else's performance so that the organization's goals and objectives are achieved. And that is how it is used most of the time. However, as manager, you not only have the responsibility to have your goals met but you also have the responsibility to ensure that the work environment is a positive one for all your direct reports. This means that you may also need to address environmental and personal concerns.

For instance, you may find that there are times when you need to coach your direct reports on issues that are not related to the actual work they do, but that definitely influence the environment and the relationships within your work group. There may be personal issues that require your attention such as attendance, tardiness, hygiene, or proper dress. Addressing these concerns falls into coaching as well.

Coaching is one of a manager's key skills for managing an employee's performance. The performance management skills of coaching (covered in this chapter) and delegating (covered in Chapter 6) will help you do what a manager is paid to do: *achieve results through and with others.*

Why Coaching Continues to Grow in Importance

In today's changing workplace, coaching is the favored strategy for developing individuals. Coaching prepares employees to broaden their responsibilities and to work more autonomously, and to take more initiative in solving problems.

❑ *Total Quality Management.* The first-line manager's role is to be a coach rather than an overseer. Coaching provides support to direct reports by helping them to develop solutions to problems, rather than by telling them what to do.

❑ *Structure of Organization.* Flat organizations have created increased areas of control so that the manager must be more of a coach than a director of specific work activities in order to accomplish all of his goals.

❑ *Staff Motivation.* Today's employees are less tolerant of an authoritative, controlling management style. As new generations come into the workplace, it will be increasingly important to pay attention to what motivates different people and to offer them the opportunities to become successful.

❑ *Organizational Changes.* Organizations are constantly changing. Coaching is particularly important in today's climate of global economy, rapid changes, heightened customer expectations, and increased competition.

Coaching Experiences

Many of you have had coaching experiences (either as the coach or the one being coached). While all coaching experiences have an impact on us in some way, individuals are especially vulnerable to coaching experiences when they are the ones being coached. Some of these experiences may have been positive, and others may have had a negative impact. The impact of a negative coaching session on an individual can be long lasting. But the benefits of a positive coaching experience are not only long lasting but also *beneficial* both to you as a manager and to your employees. The goal of this chapter is to help you become an effective coach to your direct reports so that their coaching experiences will be both positive and beneficial.

To best understand the implications of effective or ineffective coaching, think about coaching sessions you have personally had and what your response has been. Perhaps you had a manager who believed in the old fear-and-intimidation style of coaching. Or maybe your managers have been more progressive in their coaching and worked with you for your success. How did you feel after experiencing:

A Negative Coaching Experience?

_____

_____

_____

_____

_____

_____

_____

A Positive Coaching Experience?

_____

_____

_____

_____

_____

_____

_____

How would you like your direct reports to feel after they have worked with you in a coaching session? Would you like them to feel positive so that they are motivated to do the work? Learning effective coaching skills will make it possible for the outcomes of the coaching sessions to be positive.

Benefits of Coaching

We have said that coaching is an important skill for new managers. And we now know that coaching can be related to a task that needs to be accomplished, to an employee's commitment to the work she is doing, or to an environmental issue. In any case, effective coaching is a major component in creating an environment in which growth, development, and success for all can be achieved. Although coaching takes time, it can save time in the long run. When you have created a safe environment for your direct reports, so that they are comfortable talking about their development needs with you, you will have the opportunity to grow your staff members into high achievers.

Coaching is a powerful skill that can be used to maintain and improve performance and to develop new skills and enthusiasm that will help your direct reports exceed current performance and enhance their job satisfaction. When you become an effective coach, you have the ability to build a group of confident, self-motivated achievers.

Obviously, there are many benefits of coaching to all levels in an organization, or companies would not encourage their managers to take the time to learn to use this skill. Let's look at some of those benefits:

Benefits to the Organization
❑ Helps the bottom line since more work is done at a lower cost
❑ Attracts high-quality job seekers because people want to work for companies that develop their people
❑ Turnover is reduced because employees want to stay
❑ Shareholders are pleased with the improved financial statements

Benefits to You, the Manager
❑ Get the work done the way it needs to be done
❑ Have employees that want to work for you
❑ Are able to take time to do the work you need to do because your direct reports are able to do their work
❑ Have a succession plan in case you want to move to a different position
❑ Produce a better end product because of more sharing of ideas
❑ Can get more work done when people are able to do it
❑ Your stress level is reduced
❑ Take time to go to lunch or on vacation

Benefits to Your Direct Reports
❑ Feel more enthusiastic about work
❑ Will be better performers and perhaps get a higher raise

❑ Will enjoy what they do because they do it well
❑ Feel more in control of the work they do
❑ Believe that they are working for a manager who cares about them
❑ Are motivated to come to work

What Situations Will You Coach?

When the benefits are understood, and you have made a commitment to learn quality coaching, you can then consider what situations occur in your workplace about which you will actually need to coach your direct reports. There are typically four situations that require this skill, and those situations occur on a regular basis.

1. *Good-Work Coaching.* Letting people know what they do well. When you recognize good work, it will be repeated. Typically this coaching can be done on the spot and does not require the planning ahead of setting a time and location.
2. *Developmental Opportunities Coaching.* Talking to your direct reports about new opportunities that will enhance their careers through growth and development. This is the coaching that is initially used in conjunction with delegation.
3. *Poor-Work Coaching.* Letting people know what they need to do differently. Make sure that you do this in a private place with a positive approach.
4. *Poor Personal Habits Coaching.* Letting people know what they are doing that is causing problems (being late, interrupting others, poor personal hygiene) and using your best listening skills as you help them identify what is causing the problem and determine a solution.

Setting Up the Coaching Session

After you have determined that there will be a coaching meeting (this may not be required for the "good-work coaching"), taking the necessary time to plan for that meeting will have a major impact on its effectiveness. The little time this will take will pay off by providing a clear understanding of what you want to accomplish. The first consideration is logistical.

Remember to:

❏ *Set up a time* with your direct report that is convenient for both of you. It is important for both of you to be able to pay attention to the conversation. If other work or personal issues distract either person, then it will be difficult to really listen to one another.

❏ *Find a location* that is appropriate for the coaching you will be doing. If the purpose is to correct a performance problem, then it must be done in a private room.

The second consideration is mental preparedness.

❏ *Verify that your direct report is ready and willing* to be coached. There may be times when the individual does not want the news he thinks he will be getting, so he may need to be encouraged by you. One way to encourage people in this situation is to focus your request for the meeting on the benefits for the person, that is, if the person has mistakes in his work, he is required to take the time to redo it, and his performance rating will be negatively affected. Correcting the problem will speed up the work he does, and improve his rating. The person's stress level will likely be reduced with this action.

❏ *Manage yourself* so that you are able to focus on the problem/concern at hand while you are in the meeting.

When you are planning a coaching meeting, it is important to think in advance about the desired results of this meeting with your direct report. Your meeting will be more effective and have better outcomes when you plan in advance for it. Planning for these sessions will help to ensure that your goals of improving the performance of your direct reports are met.

In addition to planning your coaching meeting, it is important to utilize effective communication techniques while conducting the meeting. The following techniques will provide some suggestions on effective communication during the meeting.

Six-Step Coaching Model

The model in Figure 7-1 (beginning on next page) will assist in both the planning and conducting of your meetings.

Coaching and the Performance Management Process

Coaching and delegation are integral parts of the performance management process. As your direct reports grow in their skills and experience, you will be delegating increasingly complex tasks to them. This will require coaching them to be certain that they are able to do what you need them to do.

As a manager, you have the responsibility to be certain that all your direct reports are utilized to their fullest potential. Coaching is how you will ensure that happens.

Plan to coach your staff members regularly, whether they are performing at an exceptional level or need to improve their skills or behaviors. The Coaching Planning Worksheet provides the structure to plan for either type of a coaching meeting.

The Coaching Planning Worksheet

The Coaching Planning Worksheet (see page 127) is a tool to use in preparation for meetings with your direct reports. Take the time to answer each question before you start your coaching session. This will help you to stay on target and not be sidetracked by the individual. This focus enables you to maintain a professional position when you are feeling uncomfortable.

Figure 7-1. Six-step coaching model.

Planning Considerations	*Communication Techniques*
Step 1: Set the Stage:	
Why are you holding this meeting? ■ What instigated it? ■ Is it a problem that needs addressing? or ■ Do you want to offer your direct report an opportunity to take on some new responsibilities? ■ Perhaps you simply want to meet to check the status on annual objectives.	Clarify—Be Specific. ■ Give clear statements about perceived performance problems without using accusory language. ■ Identify the problem. ■ Outline new responsibilities. Scope the Related Problem ■ Limit statements to a single problem or two closely related problems. ■ Discuss why it is important that changes occur. Be Future-Oriented ■ State the desired change; do not request reasons for failure.
Step 2: Formulate and Focus the Issues:	
What is happening? ■ What questions will you ask to determine what is really happening or what your direct report is thinking? ■ How will you determine what the causes of any problems might be?	Promote Self-Discovery. ■ Ask questions, draw out what is happening. Discover the possibilities. Pay Attention. ■ Listen actively. Don't interrupt. Acknowledge. ■ Give verbal and nonverbal cues indicating your involvement in the conversation. Gather Information. ■ Ask questions, acknowledge, probe, reflect, and summarize.

Figure 7-1. (Continued)

Planning Considerations	Communication Techniques
Step 3: Get Agreement:	
How will you know there is agreement on the situation? ■ What will you look and listen for when discussing the situation? ■ How will you ask for agreement on the problem?	Confirm. ■ Close the loop—reach mutual agreement on problems and causes. Indicate Respect. ■ Don't use behaviors that ridicule, generalize, or judge. Affirm. ■ Comment on your direct report's strengths and positive prospects.
Step 4: Generate Possible Solutions and/or Alternatives:	
What approach will you take to meet your objectives? ■ What will you say to encourage your direct report to offer solutions? ■ Will you suggest training for improved or expanded knowledge or, perhaps, partnering with another direct report for growth?	Brainstorm. ■ Generate as many possibilities as possible. Draw Out the Consequences. ■ Weigh the upside and downside of each alternative. Decide. ■ Determine the alternative that best meets the situation.

(continues)

Figure 7-1. (Continued)

Planning Considerations	Communication Techniques
Step 5: Set Goals and Develop an Action Plan:	
What are the actions to be taken, and what are the consequences? ■ What actions will you expect your direct report to take as a result of this meeting? ■ Make sure to include some specific timelines with the actions. ■ Determine what the consequences, positive or negative, will be if your suggestions/requirements are not followed. ■ Is there a new position for the person, or will he be more prepared for a promotion?	Plan. ■ Build strategies and agree on follow-up, including milestones and timelines. Strategize. ■ Consider training, one-on-one mentoring, coaching, and resources. Recap. ■ Review key points to reinforce common understanding and ownership.
Step 6: Monitor:	
What will happen next? ■ Are there other actions that will be taken? ■ Will another meeting be scheduled?	Follow Through. ■ Set up follow-up processes, including who, when, and how.

Coaching Planning Worksheet

Employee Name _____ Meeting Date _____

Learning phase for this task/situation _____

Step 1 *Set the Stage.* Describe in detail why this meeting is being held.

Step 2 *Formulate and Focus the Issue.* What approach will you suggest to improve or enhance performance in this situation?

Step 3 *Get Agreement.* How will you get agreement from your direct report that this coaching action will be beneficial for him or her?

Step 4 *Generate Possible Solutions and/or Alternatives.* How will you encourage your direct report to brainstorm with you?

Step 5 *Set Goals and Develop an Action Plan.* With your direct report, set specific plans that include actions, timelines, and consequences, if appropriate.

Step 6 *Monitor (Next Steps).* What is your plan to follow up?

A Practice Coaching Session

Using the Six-Step Coaching Model and the Coaching Planning Worksheet, plan a coaching session for the following situation as if you were Sandy.

> ### WHAT DO I DO NOW?
>
> Sandy, Marketing Manager: The Situation as Sandy Sees It:
>
> I hired Bobby about six months ago as a marketing associate in my organization. Bobby is always bursting with ideas, but never the details. Having all the information related to a project is not a top priority for him. There is always some detail missing. When I mention this to him, he shrugs off my comments or makes a joke.
>
> During discussions, Bobby always wants to decide quickly, never giving others a chance to talk. Bobby dominates our group discussions with ideas he has developed. Others rarely have a chance to be heard. During team meetings, I am sure it is obvious to the others that I am impatient with Bobby. I have to interrupt Bobby so that others have a chance to participate and offer their ideas.
>
> Since the beginning, Bobby has been very willing to tackle new challenges and I'm pleased with that aspect of Bobby's behavior. I do wish that there would be more consideration shown for others. However, Bobby has not picked up on the group dynamics. I don't really want to confront Bobby because there are so many good attributes being displayed. But I am finding it difficult not to say something about the lack of detail and the communication skills Bobby needs to develop. I really wonder what to say and how to go about this.
>
> ❑ You are Sandy. You have decided to call Bobby in for coaching on how to work more effectively with you and the other team members.

Steps you need to take:

❑ Plan the coaching session using the planning worksheet.

❑ Use the Six-Step Coaching Model during the session.

❑ Anticipate Bobby's reaction based on what you might expect from one of your own direct reports.

Coaching Planning Worksheet

Employee Name _____ Meeting Date _____

Learning phase for this task/situation _____

Step 1 *Set the Stage.* Describe in detail why this meeting is being held.

Step 2 *Formulate and Focus the Issue.* What approach will you suggest to improve or enhance performance in this situation?

Step 3 *Get Agreement.* How will you get agreement from your direct report that this coaching action will be beneficial for him or her?

Step 4 *Generate Possible Solutions and/or Alternatives.* How will you encourage your direct report to brainstorm with you?

Step 5 *Set Goals and Develop an Action Plan.* With your direct report, set specific plans that include actions, timelines, and consequences, if appropriate.

Step 6 *Monitor (Next Steps).* What is your plan to follow up?

What Would You Do in This Situation?

Here is another case study. Read the following situation and decide how you would conduct the year-end appraisal session.

SCENARIO:

Kate has just received her yearly performance evaluation. The evaluation was done by you, her boss (with input from three of her subordinates and one peer). Your organization uses 360-degree feedback as a performance evaluation mechanism. Kate has performed satisfactorily on everything except in the area of communication. You want to send her to a three-day training program to help her develop her skills. You also want to help her by coaching her.

Steps you need to take:
❏ Plan the coaching session using the planning worksheet
❏ Use the Six-Step Coaching Model during the session
❏ Anticipate Kate's reaction based on what you might expect from one of your own direct reports.

Coaching Planning Worksheet

Employee Name _____ Meeting Date _____

Learning phase for this task/situation _____

Step 1 *Set the Stage.* Describe in detail why this meeting is being held.

Step 2 *Formulate and Focus the Issue.* What approach will you suggest to improve or enhance performance in this situation?

Step 3 *Get Agreement.* How will you get agreement from your direct report that this coaching action will be beneficial for him or her?

Step 4 *Generate Possible Solutions and/or Alternatives.* How will you encourage your direct report to brainstorm with you?

Step 5 *Set Goals and Develop an Action Plan.* With your direct report, set specific plans that include actions, timelines, and consequences, if appropriate.

Step 6 *Monitor (Next Steps).* What is your plan to follow up?

The Case of the Real Situation

Think of a situation you have back at work that will require that you do some coaching when you return to the workplace. Take a few minutes and plan for that coaching session, using the Coaching Planning Worksheet.

Consider the following in your planning:

❑ What objections will your direct report have to your coaching?
❑ What do you think her perspective will be on the situation?
❑ What attitude will she have during the coaching?
❑ What can you do to make sure that there is some receptivity to your ideas?

Coaching Planning Worksheet

Employee Name _____ Meeting Date _____

Learning phase for this task/situation _____

Step 1 *Set the Stage.* Describe in detail why this meeting is being held.

Step 2 *Formulate and Focus the Issue.* What approach will you suggest to improve or enhance performance in this situation?

Step 3 *Get Agreement.* How will you get agreement from your direct report that this coaching action will be beneficial for him or her?

Step 4 *Generate Possible Solutions and/or Alternatives.* How will you encourage your direct report to brainstorm with you?

Step 5 *Set Goals and Develop an Action Plan.* With your direct report, set specific plans that include actions, timelines, and consequences, if appropriate.

Step 6 *Monitor (Next Steps).* What is your plan to follow up?

Action Planning Notes

In order to achieve success with your performance as a manager and to have a successful team, it is important to take the time to consider what actions you will take at work. This will become the foundation for the final activity in this book.

Some examples are:
❑ Provide useful feedback on work through effective coaching.
❑ Meet with an individual to improve his or her attendance.

Which members of your team need to have their performance improved, either for a task-related need or a personal issue? When will you meet with them?

Individual	Action

CHAPTER 8

Moving Forward with Your Own Situations

Now that you have learned seven new skill areas and are wondering where to start, this chapter will give you an opportunity to think about what you want to learn about your new role as manager, and what you need to apply to improve your managerial techniques. We will approach your move forward by:

❑ Applying the tools and techniques learned in this book to the challenges in your work setting
❑ Prioritizing actions that you need to take at work
❑ Identifying the competencies on which you will focus for your personal development as a manager

Pulling Your Plans Together

Managers learning this vast array of new management skills often have a strong desire to make many changes based on the learning experienced; however, attempting to change your management behaviors all at once is unreasonable and undoable. Remember the information from the section on change in Chapter 2: Changes are best handled one at a time. Not only would you have difficulty changing many of your own behaviors but your direct reports would not know how to respond to you if you behaved completely differently.

Consequently, it is best to focus on three or four specific changes related to managing your direct reports and the work environment. Organizing and prioritizing a realistic sequence of actions and results will keep you on track for your personal development and that of your direct reports.

Using the action planning notes you have taken at the end of each chapter, and the following guidelines, formulate a specific plan of action that will produce the greatest results:

❑ Return to the highest-priority challenging situations you identified in the Introduction to this book. These will become your foundations for the actions you will identify here.
❑ Review your action planning notes from the end of each chapter.
❑ Identify the three or four actions that when taken will increase your or your direct reports' effectiveness in your challenging situations.
❑ Prioritize these actions.
❑ Identify dates when these actions will be taken (it may be a range of dates).
❑ Share your plans with a colleague at work to clarify your ideas and get additional suggestions.

Key Planned Actions from Your Planning in Each Chapter

Action	Individual(s)	Date
Priority 1		
Priority 2		
Priority 3		
Priority 4		

Index

About the Author

Carol Whitten Ellis is a partner in *Ellis Associates,* a firm providing business education and career management services. Ms. Ellis has done extensive work writing and delivering training classes for managers, and is the author for the American Management Association course Management Skills for New Managers that is the foundation of this book. Her consulting services focus on providing management development and career management support for employees and individuals specializing in the areas of management skills, interpersonal communications skills, team building, and the employee side of corporate restructuring.

Ms. Ellis holds a Bachelor of Arts degree from the University of California at Berkeley and a Master of Arts degree in career development from the John F. Kennedy University. She was a corporate manager for more than twenty years, providing sales, marketing, and regulatory direction for her teams in Pacific Bell and AT&T.

Ms. Ellis lives in Placitas, New Mexico.

You've read the book.
Now, experience the dynamic seminar!

Management Skills for New Managers

SEMINAR #2238

Take your skills even further with this powerful, best-selling seminar, led by today's top management development practitioners.

More than 70,000 new managers to date have depended on this landmark seminar as the training ground for successful careers. In just three days, you'll develop extensive skills, tools and techniques with applications based on actual day-to-day interactions with your direct reports. You'll discover how to capitalize on your strengths and those of your people. You'll learn how to take on new responsibilities with greater confidence and experience increasingly positive results. And you'll gain a deeper understanding of your role and responsibilities as an agent of both short-term and long-term success.

WHO SHOULD ATTEND
New managers with one to three years of management experience.

THE SEMINAR AT A GLANCE

- Defining Your Role and Responsibilities
- Performance Management and Appraisal
- Effective Communication: Electronic, Phone and Face-to-Face
- Capitalize on Your Employees' Natural Motivators
- Coaching for Performance
- Delegation for Growth and Development

PLUS: Go beyond the basics with...

- The New Manager Self-Assessment Tool
- Situational Leadership®II—The Art of Influencing Others*

ACTION-ORIENTED, HANDS-ON LEARNING

PRESENTATION CLASS DISCUSSION TEAM EXERCISES CASE STUDY COURSE MANUAL

For complete seminar content and schedule information, call 1-800-262-9699 or visit www.amanet.org

*Ken Blanchard's Situational Leadership® II (SLII®) is a model for developing people and a way for leaders to help their employees become self-reliant achievers. To be truly effective, leaders' styles must adapt to the skills and commitment of the people they want to influence. With some people, managers have to provide a great deal of direction. With others, encouragement and appreciation trigger the best results. Still others deliver their best when allowed to take the ball and run with it. Situational Leadership® II helps managers become more flexible and responsive to their employees' needs.